The Story of Wood

Foreign Languages Press

First Edition 2006

ISBN 7-119-04458-3
© Foreign Languages Press, Beijing, China, 2006
Published by Foreign Languages Press
24 Baiwanzhuang Road, Beijing 100037, China
Website: http://www.flp.com.cn
Email Addresses: info@flp.com.cn
                 sales@flp.com.cn
Distributed by China International Book Trading Corporation
35 Chegongzhuang Xilu, Beijing 100044, China
P.O. Box 399, Beijing, China
Printed in the People's Republic of China

Contents

Foreword

L.B. Namier, a British scholar, once told an amusing anecdote about an association founded in England in the 18th century, open to people who had visited the East. Later, finding that some people who had never been to the East had insinuated themselves into it, the association amended its articles to include "people who wish to visit the East".

Going to the East. For quite a long time it was virtually a longing of educated people in the West to visit China. However, their expectation that "China would always remain an antique country", as Lu Xun said, reflected nostalgia somewhat similar to that for ancient Greece or Rome. Moral sympathy often constitutes discrimination in a concealed way. Don't think that there is no such discrimination today. In Europe and the United States there are still many people who think that people still wear long robes and long plaits in China. Just like their predecessors, some people think that the Great Wall is a symbol of fear. Some think that people here can all do kungfu. Some others think that China is just a huge factory, or that this ancient civilization is like a piece of centuries-old porcelain ware which looks nice but is fragile. Anyway, the East is somewhat uncertain or mysterious.

Contacts between China and the West began over 1,000 years ago. In the Tang Dynasty (618-907) as many as 100,000 foreigners resided in the capital Chang'an (now Xi'an), but real records concerning such contacts began with Marco Polo in the

Yuan Dynasty (1206-1368). This traveler's era was immediately followed by the period of the Christian missionaries, starting with Matteo Ricci, during the 16th, 17th and 18th centuries. The third wave of visits to China was the period of the explorers of the Western Regions (areas west of the Yumenguan Pass, including Xinjiang and parts of Central Asia) in the late 19th century and early 20th century. In this long course of contacts, there was no lack of people who were intensely interested in China, such as Thomas Browne, William Temple, Giambattista Vico, Nicolas Malebranche, Baron de la Brede et de Montesquieu, Francois Quesnay, Francois-Marie de Voltaire, Jean-Jacques Rousseau, Victor Hugo and Romain Rolland. However, even if some of them wrote books like *On Chinese Characters and Others* (by Vico), *On the Chinese Political System, Law, Ethnics and Others* (by Montesquieu), as well as *South China in the 16th Century* and *Lettres Edifiantes et Curieuses*, none of them had a profound understanding of Chinese culture, and most of their works are nothing more than superficial informal discussions or travelers' notes on China. Later, the British admiral Lord George Anson led troops to China twice, and wrote *A Voyage Round the World*. He sharply criticized the corruption of the Chinese government and the inherent weakness of the nation (this poured

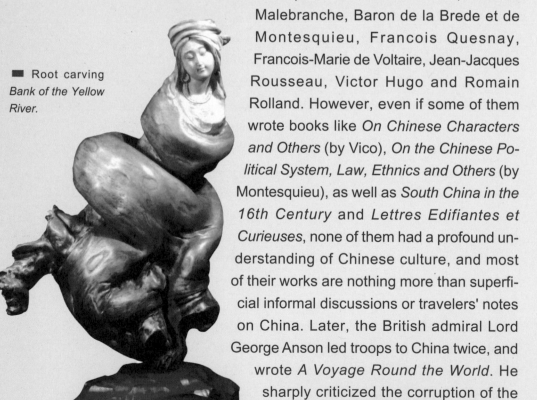

■ Root carving
Bank of the Yellow River.

■ Inscribed wooden slips dating from the Han Dynasty unearthed at Juyan, north-west China.

cold water on the "China fever" in Europe at the time, and had a considerable influence on the views of Montesquieu, Jean-Jacques Rousseau, Hegel and even Karl Marx). Nevertheless, Chinese silk, porcelain, architecture and horticulture, as well as the administration system, customs, religions and writing all began to attract the attention of Westerners, some of whom came to China with a serious purpose. One of the latter was William Chambers who con-ducted a 10-year study in Guangdong and other places, and wrote two books: *Designs of Chinese Buildings, Furniture, Dresses, Machines, and Utensils* and *A Dissertation on Oriental Gardening.* In the period 1757-1762,Chambers designed Kew Gardens in London, a garden known as one with the most distinct oriental flavor and Chinese style in Europe. Chambers' visit was followed by the unsuccessful mission to China of the first British diplomatic team led by Lord George Macartney (1737-1806).

■ The gateway to the Confucius Mansions,Qufu, Shandong.

Furniture and utensils for daily life, as well as buildings and gardens can be regarded as "entrances" to Chinese civilization. And when entering the long passageway of Chinese civilization, it was very likely that wood, like a language, played an important mediatory role. Compared with the hardness, heaviness, sturdiness and tidiness of stone buildings, wooden buildings are soft, natural, simple, affectionate, friendly, and have a more natural life taste and human appeal. Westerners use stone and make it rational and systematic, but the Chinese have wedged something called the "character of wood" deeply into their culture and lives. If one has a good understanding of this, one can have a better understanding of the Chinese tradition.

Legend has it that during the Eastern Han Dynasty (25-220), a man in Henei (north of the Yellow River in today's Henan Province) called Ding Lan often missed his parents who had died in his childhood. He carved their figures out of wood and treated them as though they were alive. Before he started eating at every meal, he offered the food first to his "parents". He used to report to them before leaving home, and greet them again after returning home. After this had gone on for a long time, Ding Lan's wife pricked the finger of one of the wooden figures with a needle, out of curiosity. To her consternation, the finger promptly shed blood. When Ding found out about this, he divorced his wife.

The Chinese would not doubt the true feelings of the man in this fable. What I want to stress is that since Chinese culture stresses wood so much, you may use the "tool" of wood to understand many aspects of Chinese culture. Wood can also be the background to an ancient Greek story: A man used a small piece of wood to make a stringed instrument, with the idea that "everything is numerals". After making repeated experiments on the instrument, he found all the elements in music. In China, in the remote past, the book *Zhuangzi* postulated another "wooden" keynote: If you cut a stick in half each day, you can keep on doing it forever.

■ Sculptured Redwood bed, Qing Dynasty.

Chapter **1**

Wood, a Favor with Man

Entrance to the East

The history of every nation has its own story about wood. Indeed, ever since the human race emerged, it seems that every tree has been obliged to record something for mankind.

Of course, much of the labor done by the trees has been neglected. The reason for this is that the trees can live longer than man. Also, man keeps moving, whereas trees stay in the same place. For a tree, even if it dies, its wooden character (or divine character) remains. Wherever a tree strikes its roots, it automatically gets into contact with the earth.

Trees, big or small, stand where they are, in either an orderly way or a scattered way. Like human beings, they believe in God. But this is often overlooked. Some trees have a specific gender, such as the date, coconut and papaya trees. One single tree does not bear fruit, but when two trees grow together, they can bear fruit. In this secret there is a complicated mechanism similar to the sexual transformation of the red snapper. Perhaps the wind, sunshine or water can know something about their secret intercourse underground.

Many of us like to sniff the smells of different tree leaves. Many kinds of trees can release a certain chemical matter when their leaves are eaten or gnawed by insects, and can help to transform linoleic acid into jasmine ketonic acid. This is very similar to the function of the prostate gland. Jasmine ketonic acid can also lure leaves to manufacture an enzyme known as a protein enzyme inhibitor which can make the leaves repugnant to insects, which would otherwise eat them. It can also help them produce a kind of hallucinogen which makes the insects feel as if they have already eaten enough, so that they fly away quickly.

The trees are closely united. When one tree is attacked or hurt, the jasmine ketonic acid releases a smell to warn the surrounding trees, so that they can all get their defense systems ready in time. Some plants can spray a poisonous fluid for self-defense when they are attacked, thanks to reflexes which help to regulate the pressure of the water inside the plants and their growth. Moreover, when the feelers of

■ An old mulberry tree on the campus of Peking University.

some plants are touched, some cells shrink automatically while others expand. As a result, the feelers show their ability to probe, twine, climb and seize. Botanists have long since become acquainted with these and other properties of trees. Therefore, they always do their best to plant together different species of trees which they feel can become friends. This, at least, is much safer than planting one species of trees over a large area. Like human beings, when trees of the same species grow together for a long time, their resistance to or accommodation with their surroundings becomes slow.

The ancients thought that trees had a mysterious connection with the spirits. For instance, there is a tree called the peepul or bo tree. It was introduced from India to China, where it is called "Guijianchou", meaning "ghosts are afraid at the sight of it". A Buddhist classic recommends cutting down one of these trees, and burning it while reciting a certain incantation 21 times in order to dispel ghosts and demons. In the *Annotations to Ancient and Modern Textual Research* by Cui Bao, it is recorded that a sorcerer called Bao Mao uses a stick made from this kind of tree to beat and drive away ghosts. To date, wood from this kind of trees is used for making Buddhist rosary beads.

Eaglewood is also regarded by the Buddhists as a tree with supernatural properties.

In the ancient Chinese text called the *Book of Mountains and Seas*, the brothers Shen Tu and Yu Lei drove ghosts back to the Underworld through a hole in a peach tree. This led to the custom of carving images of the brothers out of peach tree wood and hanging them in front of the door on the eve of the Spring Festival, to deter the entrance of evil spirits. This is the origin of the later custom of hanging Spring Festival couplets outside the house. Moreover, this notion of the peach tree being a talisman against evil spirits is reflected in the habit of referring to the central room of a house (from which a deceased person was thought to ascend to Heaven) as the "peach room" in some parts of China even today.

Wooden Houses

As we go back in time, we discover that wood was used to make paper, and that wooden blocks were the first printing implements. The first records were made by incising marks on trees. Further back, the first seeds were planted in the ground after using a pointed wooden stick to make the holes for them.

Building materials in China were traditionally mainly wood. Even when other materials such as stone were used, the ornamentation is often in imitation of wooden structures.

The affinity and sense of security given by wood cannot be replaced by other things. From trees to wood, it

■ Wooden cottages of the Yao ethnic group, Longsheng County, Guangxi Zhuang Autonomous Region.

was also a natural and living ecology even in the instinct of the most primitive aesthetic thinking. Even in the sunken dwellings of primitive man found in Banpo in Xi'an, Beishouling in Baoji, Mount Yuanchang in Longdongzhen and Mengge Village in Hebei, wooden stakes held up the roofs, which were held in place by wooden rafters.

One of the advantages of a wooden structure is its ability to withstand the shock of an earthquake. For example, the 67.3-meter-high wooden pagoda in the Fogong Temple in Yingxian County, Shanxi Province, which was built in 1065 and is the oldest and tallest wooden tower extant in China, has withstood numerous earthquakes.

The traditional roof of Chinese buildings has upturned eaves, which make it look large but at the same time light and airy, as if it is about to fly away. The curved surface of

■ Wooden pagoda, Liao Dynasty, in Yingxian County, Shanxi Province.

the roof enables the wind to scud from its surface and rain-drops to flow off immediately. Speaking of the canopy, the *Book of Rites* of the Zhou Dynasty says, "The above should be high and the below should be low. This formation can let water run off quickly." The "above" and "below" refer to Heaven, Earth and Man in another sense, and this is a topic we will discuss repeatedly in this book.

Worship of a Single Log

Wooden houses are more comfortable than caves. They are also environmentally friendly, warm, and earthquake- and sound-proof.

The Chinese have a great fondness for wood. They like one-piece wooden furniture, and even a single log for a coffin.

People of the Li ethnic group in south China's Hainan Province make all their utensils out of single pieces of wood — from dug-out canoes to rice bowls. No alien materials, such as nails, are used, although the mor-tise-and-tenon technique can be seen occasionally.

■ Fossil wood in the Imperial Garden of the Forbidden City.

The Story of Wood

These utensils are divided into two categories: daily-use utensils and production tools. The former group includes rice-husking mortars, chairs and bowls, while the latter hoes, plows, shuttles, dugout canoes and ox-driven carts. Besides, pig troughs, drums, scabbards and statues of deities are all made from single logs.

Nanmu and some other local species of trees are preferred for making utensils. The trunks are first soaked in water for two or three months until they emit a heavy smell of mud. This is to ensure that they are insect-proof.

Legend has it that the Li people's ancestors came to Hainan Island in dugout canoes, and to this day their houses are said to resemble upturned canoes. When banyan trees are used for making dugouts, first the bark is stripped off, and then iron chisels are used to cut out an oblong space in the

■ Dugout canoes still used by the Li people.

log. A slow fire then burns in the hollow place, and the burnt wood is cut away. This process is repeated until the desired shape emerges.

Wood as the Foundation

After our ancestors left the caves, they had been dwelling in for countless millennia. They naturally turned to wood to build houses for themselves. The most ancient of such dwellings have been discovered at Banpo, which all face the south, as do modern Chinese houses. Using wood for the frame and grass for the roof, this style of housing foretold that the Chinese people would use wood as the foundation for their buildings for a very long time to come.

In the course of working with wood, they accidentally discovered that fire could be made by drilling hard wood with a pointed wooden stick. Trees provided another support for their livelihood. Starting with wood, the ancient Chinese created their world outlook which postulated that everything was composed of interactive elements of wood, water, fire, earth and metal. Thus the starting point for philosophy in China was different from that of the West, where stone monuments were the earliest structures.

Chinese architecture prefers wood due to its properties of identical center, fine grain, close texture, soft color and close ties to man. Wood did not seem to die. When it fell down, it stood up again, and grew again in the artificial dimensions of space and time.

■ Calligraphy on wooden boards in the Chinese characters of plum, orchid, bamboo and chrysanthemum.

The use of wood constrained the size of ancient buildings. The interior of a building could not be boundlessly spacious, like the stone-built Gothic architecture of the West, which gives prominence to a big enclosed space. The interiors of ancient Chinese buildings were designed to house all kinds of decorations, tables, chairs, screens, winding corridors and halls — everything full of human interest. Each detail has its own flavor and is a minor element serving the purport of the main body. The internal space is limited, but it can be enlarged by artificial decoration and refurnishing.

As they were limited in height, Chinese ancient buildings could only be expanded horizontally. This trend has exerted major influences on the Chinese nation's architectural style and structure of thinking. The use of wood as the foundation of buildings helped to develop the space and even the external form of humanity. Besides, it also gave birth to another exotic flower of the national art of architecture — horticulture. Chinese gardens show the greatest possible harmony between man and nature. Hills, waters, tree shadows, clouds, river waves, small bridges, flowing water, chirping birds, smoke from cooking fires, pavilions, and even distant landscapes were included in the artificial layouts.

When the Chinese apply paint to brick walls, or buy a set of expensive mahogany furniture, or take up a wooden plaything, we know that it is because they have been close to wood since they are born.

Chapter **2**

Carpenters

Lun Bian and His Carriage

The Taoist mystic Zhuangzi told a famous story about a carpenter: One day, Duke Huan of the State of Qi was reading a book, while Lun Bian was making wheels for a carriage nearby. Lun Bian asked, "What book are you reading?" Duke Huan replied, "A book written by a sage." Lun Bian asked again: "Is the sage still alive?" The answer was that he had died long ago. Lun Bian said with a sigh, "What you are

■ Light horse-drawn carriage of the late Western Han Dynasty, designed based on the concepts of round heaven and square earth, unearthed at Pengjiazhai, Xining, Qinghai Province.

reading is nothing more than the dross of the ancients." Duke Huan, annoyed, asked the carpenter what he meant, and the latter replied, "When I am making a wheel, if the tenon is too small, it can be easily inserted into the mortise, but the wheel will be not firm. If the tenon is too big, it cannot be inserted into the mortise. Therefore, the tenon must be neither small nor big. It must be fit exactly. But the real knack of this cannot be told in words, and I can't even explain it clearly to my own son. So if the ancients and their skills that cannot be passed down are already dead, even the most profound truth cannot be explained clearly in books. Therefore, the book you are reading is nothing more than the dross of the ancients."

This was a famous carpenter in Chinese history. He was famous because he unconsciously spoke of the extremely important "wheel" in aesthetics, namely, the circle. Every detail of a house, for example, the circular shape, the oblong shape, the vase-shaped doorsill, and the window frames in the shape of banana leaves, peaches, overlapped water melons or fans get inspiration from it.

The training of a carpenter was bound to affect all aspects of folk tradition. Chopping or chiseling, light or heavy, beautiful or crude, exquisite or rustic, they are all the result of the combination of skilful hands and the mind. Furniture has always been not only simple furniture, but a kind of nature, a kind of construction and simulation. Of course, it was not training in a given time and a given place that produced fine objects, but the naturally possessed sensitiveness to all things around the carpenters in nature. Whatever is made looks like whatever is wanted. This is the most essential requirement for a carpenter. Of course, the system and cultural customs passed down by their ancestors streamlined

The Story of Wood

■ Carpenter's tools unearthed from a Han Dynasty
tomb in Tianchang County, Anhui Province.

the work of carpenters in one direction. This has helped develop a common memory of folk customs, as well as promoting professional innovation and involvement. Take the image of the bat for example. It has been used as a decorative motif because its curved wings can be incorporated into many different patterns. In addition, the character "蝠" in its name "蝙蝠" has the same pronunciation as the character "福" in the word 幸福 (happiness). Therefore, in the hands of the carpenter, the bat became a symbol of happiness.

The finest carpenters all seem to have a "connecting line" of the hands, eyes and mind of a nation, the overflow of the feelings, the simulation of Nature and the creation of aesthetics. Chiseling, planing, chopping, cutting, judging, carving, polishing, and rules and standards — all these techniques have been established step by step.

Master Carpenter Lu Ban

Lu Ban is regarded as the founding father of carpentry in China. His family name was Gongshu, and his given name was Ban. He was also known as Gongshuzi（公输子）, Gongshu Pan, Ban Shu and Lu Ban. As "般" and "班" are both pronounced "ban", later generations called him Lu Ban. He was born in the third year (507 BC) of the reign of Duke Ding of the State of Lu. The date of his death is unknown.

Lu Ban lived in the years that saw the changeover from the Spring and Autumn Period (770-476 BC) to the Warring States Period (475-221 BC). He had been a slave, but because of his skill he was made a free man, and put in charge of large construction projects.

Commissioned to build a large palace, he grew impatient with the slowness of the method of cutting timber with axes. One day, he accidentally cut his hand on a blade of grass. He

■ Depiction of Master Carpenter Lu Ban.

observed the blade of grass closely, and saw that they had sawtooth edges. This led him to invent the saw. The first saws he made were of bamboo, which wore out quickly, and then he had saws made of iron.

Lu Ban also invented the plane, to make wooden boards flat and smooth. Another of his inventions was the carpenter's square, which is still called Lu Ban's square today. When Lu Ban used an inked string to mark straight lines, his mother held one end of it. Later, Lu Ban devised to hold one end of the line on the wood he was inking. Carpenters of later generations called this hook "Ban's mother". Moreover, the vice used to hold wood while it is being planed is called "Ban's wife".

■ Wooden cow, late Western Han Dynasty or early Eastern Han Dynasty, unearthed at Mozhuizi, Gansu Province.

Lu Ban's superb skills led to many exaggerated tales of his inventions. It is said that he once made a bird out of bamboo, which could fly by the force of wind without landing for three days. Another story has it that he built a carriage with a wooden horse and a wooden driver, which could proceed by itself. This latter story prompted many master craftsmen of later generations to try to emulate this achievement, without success. They included the machine inventor Ma Jun in the Three Kingdoms period (220-280) — represented as Zhuge Liang in the classical novel *The Romance of the Three Kingdoms*, Ou Chun of the Jin Dynasty (1115-1234), Ling Zhao of the Northern Qi Dynasty (550-577), Ma Shifeng of the Tang Dynasty (618-907) and Huang Luzhuang of the Qing Dynasty (1644-1911).

Sometime after 450 BC, Lu Ban went to the State of Chu, where he invented several devices used in warfare, including a naval grappling hook. It is said that when news that Lu Ban was working on the design of a ladder to be used to scale the wall of a besieged city came to the philosopher Mozi, the latter hurried to Chu in an attempt to dissuade him. The two of them argued heatedly about military tactics, from which Mozi emerged the winner.

Besides being a thinker, Mozi was also an inventor and a scientist. He was also a skilful craftsman. It is said that he once used a log to make a carriage axle which could bear a weight of 300 kg.

Carpenters in Folklore

The Taoist sage Zhuangzi once told a story about how a bricklayer in Ying, capital of the State of Chu, painted the tip of his nose with a thin layer of plaster no bigger than the wing of a fly. He then asked his friend, a carpenter named Shi, to chop the plaster off his nose with his axe. Shi swung his axe and chopped the piece of plaster off the bricklayer's nose, without doing any harm to his friend.

■ Carved wooden doors, Ming Dynasty.

Later, Song Yuanjun asked Shi to do it again for him, but the latter demurred, saying, "It is true that I did it once. But my friend is no longer alive, and there is nobody who can cooperate with me so well."

Zhuangzi told another story about a carpenter named Zi Qing. Zi Qing was good at making a bell-shaped ancient musical instrument called "ju" out of wood. The ju he made amazed everyone who saw them, and they praised Zi Qing's superb craftsmanship. When the Duke of the State of Lu asked him the secret of his art, Zi Qing answered, "I have no special ability; I have only experience. Before I start to make a ju, I bathe and fast, and get rid of distracting thoughts. On the third day of fasting and bathing, all distracting thoughts of celebrating victories, being offered an official post and receiving a fat salary have vanished. On the fifth day, all remarks made by others for or against me are forgotten. On the seventh day, I even forget myself. Then, I go into the mountains and forests to observe the texture of the trees, and carefully choose the material whose natural form is ideal for making ju. It is only when a complete ju has been formed in my mind that I begin to work on it. In fact, the method is a combination of my natural instinct and the natural instinct of the wood. This is why my ju can be called a superb work."

The way employed by the carpenter is to turn himself into a wise man using carpenter's tools. Of course, it includes some brain work, some stratagem, some trick, and some professional secrets unknown to the outsiders, and even miscellaneous and secretive taboos and rituals. For example, a carpenter dislikes his tools being touched by others. When felling a tree, it is the custom to leave some uncut pieces of wood on the stump, because this is believed to represent a

Court furniture, Qing Dynasty.

"memorial tablet to the tree".

Carpenters' skills in building houses and furniture are highly prized among the people. It is precisely for this reason that the ceremony for apprenticeship to a master carpenter has always been very solemn. The esoteric ceremonies that accompany apprenticeship are designed to instill the right attitude and dedication into the beginning carpenter.

An interesting fact is that many masters of traditional Chinese painting were also good at carpentry. Zhao Ji of the Song Dynasty (1082-1135), who later became the emperor, was fond of practicing calligraphy and painting before he ascended the throne. In the third year of his reign (1104), he formally included Chinese painting as part of the imperial examinations, and required mastery of six genres, namely, Buddhist themes, figures, landscapes, birds and beasts, flowers and bamboos, and the decoration of wooden houses. One of the most noted painters of contemporary times, Qi Baishi, also learned carpentry in his early years, and changed to painting later.

Apart from ordinary carpenters, the imperial courts of all dynasties had their own carpenters, who were called "palace carpenters". Many masterpieces of sandalwood carvings which have been passed down from ancient times are extant today.

Chapter **3**

Traditional Buildings

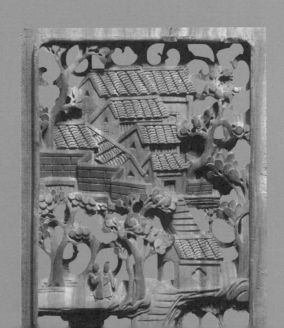

The Earliest Use of Wood

In the earliest times, our ancestors all lived in natural rock caves. Such caves dating from the Old Stone Age are found in the areas of Beijing, and Liaoning, Guizhou, Guangdong, Hubei, Jiangxi, Jiangsu and Zhejiang provinces. In the north, the first ones to be inhabited were natural caves; then artificial caves were carved out; and finally buildings were constructed in the open.

In the south, people used wood right from the very beginning, probably because there was an abundance of wood there in those days. It is said in the book *Hanfeizi*

26

■ Shang Dynasty palace restored on the original pillar bases in light of historical records.

that "In ancient times, there were few people, but many birds and beasts, and the people could not defeat the birds, beasts, insects and snakes. A sage spoke of using wood to build shelters against their attacks."

Differences of regional geography and culture gave rise to differences in the styles of buildings erected. For example, there were bamboo houses on piles, called locally as 干阑 "ganlan" (elevated houses) in the hot and damp hilly regions of Yunnan Province, south China. In the north, the nomadic ethnic minorities live in felt tents, which could be easily dismantled and moved elsewhere. Cave dwellings have lasted until today in the loess soil areas along the Yellow River. In the forest areas of northeast and northwest China, log cabins are still common.

Remains of wooden houses have been found at some of the most ancient prehistoric sites in China — Hemudu in Yuyao, Zhejiang Province, Banpo Village, near Xi'an, and Erlitou, southwest of Yanshi in Henan.

During the Shang and Zhou dynasties, Chinese architecture was already beginning to show some of the characteristics which later came to be regarded as uniquely Chinese, such as orderly and regular courtyards, layout with a symmetrical vertical axis, and a structural system with wood

■ Wood carving depicting a courtyard dwelling.

beams forming the framework. At that time, most of the larger main buildings had wooden frameworks, and the walls were made of adobe. Under the front and rear eaves, eave pillars were planted in rammed-earth foundations. During the Warring States Period, large-scale construction was undertaken in all states, and all palaces consisted of wooden pavilions built on terraces of rammed earth. The capital cities of various states were usually divided into an inner city, where the court and its officials were located, and an outer city where ordinary citizens resided.

In the more than 1,000 years from the Warring States Period to the decline of the Northern and Southern Dynasties, wood played an increasingly important role in construction. Lattice windows and herringbone arches were added to the basic structures of side wings, xuanshan (overhanging gable roof), xieshan (gable and hip roof), zanjian and dunding (flat-vaulted roof). The unification of China in the Qin Dynasty in 221 BC and the subsequent consolidation of standard methods of architecture in the following Western Han Dynasty (206 BC-220 AD) led to an amalgamation of various styles of buildings that had prevailed in various part of the country. During the Wei, Jin and Northern and Southern Dynasties (220-589), the cultures of many different ethnic groups were further blended, and Buddhism saw its heyday in China. Buddhist pagodas emerged in great numbers, all built of wood. At first, they were copied from those in India, but they gradually assumed the distinctive Chinese style of later centuries.

Characteristics of Ancient Buildings

The oldest extant wooden structures in China date from the Tang Dynasty (618-907), which saw the maturity of Chinese architecture. We can only know about buildings before that period from archeological ruins, and paintings, carvings and other artistic works. However, this has not hindered us from roughly summarizing the major characteristics of ancient Chinese architecture:

1. Wood was always the principal building material. Thus, wood determined the unique structural form of traditional Chinese buildings.

2. The truss principle was universal, with combinations of posts, beams and crossbeams.

3. The corbel bracket is a Chinese contribution to architecture, and its practical and aesthetic values cannot

■ Columns of the Temple of Heaven, Beijing.

be underestimated. It is a projecting structure of tier of short blocks and trapezoid blocks suspended outside the main structure. At first, it was a transitional part inserted between the top of a pillar and a beam, but gradually it developed into an integral part of the building.

4. Standardization of individual buildings. The ancient Chinese palaces, temples and houses were all groupings of individual buildings. Each building consisted of three parts: the foundation with steps, the main body, and the roof. The foundation was built of bricks or natural stones. On it, the main body of the building was erected, with wood pillars as the skeleton, interspersed with doors, windows and partitions for ventilation. The surface of the roof was usually gently and elegantly curved, and covered with greenish glazed tiles. The roof was likened to a light and elegant crown.

■ Wooden drum tower in Sanjiang County, Guangxi Zhuang Autonomous Region.

■ Depiction of an old
entrance to a garden.

Individual buildings were usually rectangular, but they could also be square, octagonal or even circular.

5. The layout was multi-tiered, with the accent on the maximum balance and symmetry. Reflecting the hierarchical nature of traditional Chinese society, there is a fixed arrangement of buildings in a group according to seniority in age, generation and rank of the inhabitants. For example, the main building in an architectural ensemble is the principal center of activities for the head of the household, and the side buildings are all a bit lower in form, decoration and attachments. A group of buildings always had at least one courtyard, and large mansions had several or even a dozen courtyards. Also, the individual buildings were grouped around a central axis.

6. The layout was very flexible. The partitions, doors, screens and other auxiliary facilities for dividing up the space inside a traditional Chinese building were made so that they could be dismantled and rearranged in other combinations at any time.

7. Paint was used from the earliest times to protect the wood from insects, cracking, dry rot, etc. This led to extensive use of colored paintings to decorate the buildings. Such painting developed into a distinctive genre of its own, with fanciful designs relying heavily on mythology and symbols.

■ The Hunan-Guangdong Guild Hall, Beijing.

Timber for Official Buildings

Very simple and tersely bold outlines and artistic decoration of ancient rusticity marked the architecture of the Han Dynasty. In the Tang Dynasty, a multiplicity of architectural styles were blended equally, resulting in imposing and neat, open and natural buildings. We can still see from paintings and other artistic works, as well as the structure of corbel brackets and the images of the pillars and beams that by the time art had already been integrated with architecture. All this reflected the splendid prosperity of the Tang Dynasty.

The "Tang fashion" continued through the Liao, Jin and Western Xia dynasties (907-1234). However, the Liao Dynasty saw the combination of Tang tradition and the craftsmanship of northern tribes. An example is the wooden pagoda in the Fogong Temple in Yingxian County, Shanxi Province.

The Song Dynasty marked another milestone in the development of Chinese architecture. During this dynasty, the search for the so-called "heavenly principles" dominated intellectual life. This search entailed "eradicating human desires" and a return to Confucian orthodoxy. Based on this, the government of the Song Dynasty issued the *Rules of Architecture*, which was a complete summary of building design and technical experience. It set strict rules for every aspect of architecture, including monolithic pillars and large spaces for official buildings. This work had a far-reaching —

and negative — influence on future trends in architecture, as its stereotypes cramped the initiative of future building designers.

The creativity of architects and related craftsmen was then diverted to the gardens of houses and public buildings. Gardens became the most vigorous part of the architecture of the Northern and Southern Song dynasties and were much appreciated by scholars as their popular meeting places.

■ Joiner work of the Jin Dynasty in the main hall of the Jingtu Temple, Yingxian County, Shanxi Province.

The *Rules of Architecture* of the Northern Song Dynasty were supplemented during the Qing Dynasty (1644-1911) by an official document called *Regulations of Construction Works of the Ministry of Works of the Great Qing*. There were explicit rules for the roof truss (deciding on the slope and parabola of the roof), the outward-inclined foot of each pillar, the formation of the upward curve of a cornice, and also correcting the optical distortion in pillars by changing the normal straight line into a mild curve.

It was characteristic of Chinese culture that, while literary pursuits such as the writing of essays and poems were honored and such works produced in abundance, there was always a scarcity of blueprints and working drawings. Indeed, apart from the *Rules of Architecture* and the *Regulations of Construction Works of the Ministry of Works of the Great Qing*, there were almost no textbooks on architecture at all in China. The reformer Liang Qichao of the late Qing Dynasty sent copies of these two works to his son Liang Sicheng, who was studying architecture at Harvard University and later became a prestigious architect.

Structural Carpentry

Structural carpentry is traditionally divided into small and large items. The former were divided into 12 categories, including the bracket, baulk trapezoid block, ang and locust head. The other eight items are as follows:

1. Pillar. Pillar is an upright member bearing weight from above. Their sections are generally circular. They are the solidest members in a building. The outer pillars are called eave pillars, and the inner ones are called internal pillars. Those in the corners are called corner pillars. Not all pillars stand straight. Some, tilting slightly toward the center as a whole, are called "side feet".

Detail of an ornate roof support.

2. Architrave. Architraves include column tie (major and minor beams), plate architrave, interior column-top tie, ground sill, short subordinate beam (later known as a sparrow brace, or queti), and a horizontal member connecting the tops or feet of two pillars. This is also called "tiao".

3. Beam. In an ordinary house, there must be a horizontal member to bear the weight of the roof. This is the function of the beam. There are several layers of beams. Generally speaking, the upper beams are shorter than the lower ones, and the combination of the beams forms the roof truss. The lowest beam is placed on the top of the pillars or combined with the bracketing unit. The beams are named according to their lengths: The one-rafter-long beam is called daqian, the two-rafter-long beam is called rufu, or small beam or eave beam (double-span beam), the four-rafter-long beam is called sichuanfu, or five-purlin beam, and the eight-rafter-long beam

is called bachuanfu, or nine-purlin beam. The uppermost beam is called pingliang, or top beam (three-purlin beam), on which is a short post or column (spine column) to bear the hip rafter (ridge truss). The exposed beam under the ping'an, or tianhua (plain lattice ceiling), is called mingfu or exposed beam. The latter is divided into straight beams and crescent beams, according to their external forms. The straight beams are straight on all sides, while the crescent beams are bent like bows. The purlin parallel to the beam placed between two pillars (columns) and under the lowest beam is called shunfuchuan, or along-beam tie. During the Ming and Qing dynasties, the purlin closely placed under the beam was called suiliang fang.

4. Midge post, humped support, and diagonal brace. All these are members on the frames and beams. In early construction, short posts, camel's hump or duntian, and over-bay-straining ties were erected on the beams to bear the head of the beam above. A support was placed diagonally on the beam head, and the rafters (purlins) were placed on the diagonal supports. The midge posts and braces were placed on the top beams. Short posts were used on the beams of all official constructions in the Ming and Qing dynasties, called "upper golden squat queen posts," "lower golden squat queen posts" and "ridge squat queen post," according to their positions. Corner ridges were used under all posts. When ridge rafters were lengthened for the pushing-out gable of a side building, another top beam was added under the rafter heads. It was called a taiping (peace) beam, and the post erected on the beam was called the thunder-god post.

5. Wooden strip, or ti timber. This was used mainly in the Tang Dynasty and abandoned gradually later. It was used

under the joints of two members, parallel to the rafters and purlins. Its function was to increase the strength of the joints and shorten the span.

6. Rafters and over-bay-straining ties. The rafter is a vertical member to bear battens and connect the horizontal purlins and beams. A rafter with a circular section is simply called a rafter, and that with a rectangular section is called a rafter bearer. Its length is calculated as the length of the battens (plus the projecting tenon) and the length of the outrigger. For example, at the corner of a house, a triangular block is often added on the back of the rafter to make the roof curved slightly upwards. The over-bay-straining tie is used under the rafter, linking the purlins and beams to strengthen the structural integrity.

7. Corner beam, or Yangma. This is usually used on the 45° lines of the returns of the side building roofs or gable-and-hip roofs, and placed at the nodes of the front and side faces of frame rafters. Major corner beams (or senior corner beams) are used at the bottom, and junior corner beams are used to bear the rafter tails at the corners of the roof.

8. Rafter, or feizi. The section of a rafter is circular. Its head and tail are nailed to the top and bottom purlins, respectively. Each horizontal length, i.e. , the bay of the purlin, is called one rafter or one jia or one bujia. If overhanging eaves are used, a feizi with a rectangular section is nailed on the eave rafter.

Folk Arts and Crafts

Architecture uses the language of the three-dimensional or even four-dimensional space in which a man lives and moves. Inside it are not only the tangible parts of materials, structure, modeling and decorations, but also the not directly visible rules, laws and crafts.

Architecture is the art of creating spaces, namely, how to turn the useless parts into the most useful. This is perhaps why, traditionally, master carpenters have been regarded as possessing almost magical powers in China. Many people would say that carpenters could see "ghosts" or deities when a new beam was put into place in a house, or see a mysterious shadow when they made a coffin.

■ Carved wooden windows, Republic of China period, Huizhou.

■ Qing Dynasty sacrificial
table made of nanmu wood.

Because official buildings, such as palaces, and the houses and other structures tended to follow the rigid rules laid down in the two handbooks mentioned above, it is among the minority peoples that we find the creativity and originality of the ancient Chinese people. For example, the wooden houses of the Lisu people are built of simple materials like bamboo, wood, mud, grass and stone slabs. The houses look like big wooden boxes. Round logs five meters long with an average diameter of 20 cm form the lintels, and wooden planks form the roof. The walls are built of round logs of the same length, one piled upon the other, to form rectangles. The four walls are raised from the ground to support the beam of the house. Not a single nail is used for the whole house, which is referred to as a "seamless heavenly robe".

Chapter **4**

Visits to Palaces

Epang and Weiyang Palaces

The Divine Altar, the Divine Pond and the Divine Farm were special structures built in ancient China. They represented, respectively, the mountains, lakes and other waterways, and the land and its products. They symbolized the authority of the emperor over "all under Heaven".

When the first emperor of the Qin Dynasty, Qin Shi Huang, unified China, he consciously absorbed the architectural styles and technical experience of all the six states he had unified, and had palaces built along the banks of the Jinghe and Weihe rivers around Xianyang, in present-day Shaanxi Province. Duke Huiwen of the State of Qin built a palace, but he did not finish the work before his death, and his successor, the first emperor of the Qin Dynasty, completed the construction.

This was the Epang Palace, and wood was its main material. Through a skilful combination of a rammed earth foundation and wooden framework, the builders achieved an artistic effect of grandeur. Later, a soothsayer told Qin Shi Huang that he should have more palaces built, so that he could live forever, by moving from one to the other invisibly.

The emperor started work on another palace, called Shanglin Gardens, but he died before it could be completed. Emperor Wu of the succeeding Han Dynasty completed the work.

A large number of such palaces, called "Gardens of Immortals", were built during the Qin and Han dynasties, including the following: Yichun Garden, Leyou Garden, Yusu Garden, Sixian Garden, Bowang Garden and Kunwu Garden. Even more luxurious than these were labyrinthine palaces named Jianzhang, Chengguang, Chuyuan, Baoyang, Guangyange, Wangyuan, Quantai, Xuanqu, Zhaotai, Fuli and Putao. There were Taoist temples and pools in the gardens and palaces, such as Kunming Temple, Jianguan Temple, Pingle Temple, Yuanwang Temple, Yankai Temple, Guanxiang Temple, Bailu Temple, Yanglu Temple, Yangde Temple and Yuliao Temple. The pools included Kunming Pool, Michi Pool, Niushou Pool, Kuaichi Pool, Jicao Pool, Dongbei Pool, Xibei Pool, Danglu Pool, Taiyi Pool and Langchi Pool. It is said that there were more than 3,000 species of fruit trees, exotic flowers, grasses and other plants in these Shanglin Gardens.

■ Empress Dowager Cixi's bedroom.

A Glimpse of Major Palaces

The extravagance in the Qin and Han dynasties struck the keynote for the emperors of the subsequent dynasties. The Weiyang Palace, built for an emperor of the early Han Dynasty, had an enclosing wall of 8,900 meters. The emperors of various dynasties all vied with their predecessors in the extravagance of palatial constructions. Apart from the above-mentioned Epang and Weiyang palaces, the famous ancient Chinese palaces included the following:

Changle Palace (also called the Eastern Palace historically). It was rebuilt by Liu Bang, Emperor Gaozu of the Han Dynasty, on the basis of the Xingle Palace built in the Qin Dynasty. Serving as the political center of the Western Han Dynasty, it consisted of the Changxin Hall, the Changqiu Hall, the Yongshou Hall and the Yongning Hall.

■ Restoration of part of the Xianyang Palace of the Qin Dynasty.

Jianzhang Palace. Emperor Wu of the Western Han Dynasty built the Guigong Palace, Beigong Palace and Mingguang Palace. He also built the Jianzhang Palace in the western part of the capital, Chang'an, and expanded the Shanglin Gardens of the Qin Dynasty in the southwestern part of the city, excavated the Kunming Lake, and built temporary residences for himself in other places.

Daming Palace. Li Shimin, Emperor Taizong of the Tang Dynasty, built the Yong'an Palace at Longshouyuan in the northeastern corner of Chang'an in 634, as a summer resort for his father Li Yuan. Li Yuan died before the work was completed. In the following year, the palace was renamed Daming Palace. It was rebuilt in the second year (662) of the Longshuo reign period, and renamed Penglai Palace. It was the political center throughout the rest of the Tang Dynasty.

Potala Palace. Located on Maburi Hill, in the northwest of Lhasa, capital of the Tibet Autonomous Region, is 3,700 meters above sea level and has nine levels. It was built in the seventh century as the headquarters of the rule by politics-religion (Lamaism) integration in Tibet and the winter residence of the Dalai Lamas.

■ The Potala Palace in Lhasa, Tibet Autonomous Region.

The Imperial Palace in Shenyang. This palace was built by Nurhachi, Emperor Taizu of the Qing Dynasty, in 1625. After the death of Nurhachi, Huangtaiji, his son, completed the construction. Covering an area of more than 60,000 square meters, the palace was built in imitation of the Forbidden City in Beijing.

Yonghegong Lamasery. This construction bears the architectural characteristics of the Han, Manchu, Mongolian and Tibetan ethnic groups. Located in Beijing, it was the

■ The Yonghegong Lamasery in Beijing.

residence of Qing Dynasty Emperor Yongzheng (reigned 1723-1736) before he ascended to the throne. It later became a major place of worship of Tibetan Lamaism. It is now also a tourist attraction.

Forbidden City. Located in the center of Beijing, it is the largest and the most complete and most exquisite palatial construction in China. Its construction began in the fourth year (1406) of the Yongle reign period of the Ming Dynasty and was completed in the 18th year of the same reign. It was the residence and seat of government of 24 emperors of the Ming and Qing dynasties. The Taihe Hall (Hall of Supreme Harmony) is the largest wooden structure in China, with 84 pillars outside and inside. They are called "panlong" columns (columns with twined dragons). Each has a diameter of more than one meter. All painted red and gilded, the pillars stand 14.5 meters from ground to the lowest beam. They are all made from precious nanmu wood transported from Yunnan, Guizhou, Sichuan and Hunan provinces. The Forbidden City measures 760 meters from east to west, and 960 meters from north to south, covering 720,000 square meters. It is divided into two parts — the outer court, where the emperors handled administrative affairs, and the inner court, where the emperors and their entourage lived. The Gate of Heavenly Purity was the dividing line between the outer and inner courts.

The outer court consists mainly of the Hall of Supreme Harmony, the Hall of Central Harmony and the Hall of Preserving Harmony. Prominence is given to the Hall of Supreme Harmony (popularly called the Hall of Golden Chimes), where the emperors held audiences.

Traditional Roofs

The roofs of traditional Chinese buildings are often the first things that impress a visitor from abroad. These roofs are shaped like the Chinese character 人 (man). They are divided into the following categories: hipped roof, gable and hip roof, overhanging gable roof, flush gable roof, juanpeng, zanjian, helm roof, single slope roof, flat-vaulted roof, flat roof, spherical calotte, vault, dome, gable roof and fantail roof. These are the varieties of roofs found on large structures. There are many more forms of roofs and combinations to be found on smaller buildings.

■ Upturned double eaves of the Hall of the Goddess in the Jinci Temple, Shanxi Province.

There were clear-cut rules for the design and construction of traditional Chinese roofs. One was the Chinese innovation of upturned eaves, which relieved the ponderous impression the roof would otherwise give. For the same reason, there are almost no straight lines on these roofs. Philosophically, the graceful curves produce the effect of motion and stillness alternating, and the void and the solid complementing each other.

Height, Colors and Grades

The units of wooden structures are restricted by the natural length of the timber used. Whether the supported-beam technique or the column-and-tie technique is used, the dimensions of the rooms are limited. The height of the largest extant hall is 30 meters, and the height of multi-story wooden pagodas had to be kept within strict limits.

Since the height could not be further raised, people could only think of how to use the ground space, and gradually formed the unwritten rule that the height should be linked with the ground layout plan.

The *Book of Wood* is said to have been the first manual on wooden structures in Chinese history. The only reference to it, however, is in the *Dream Brook Notes* by Shen Kuo, a scientist of the Northern Song Dynasty (960-1126). The *Book of Wood* set detailed rules for different parts of buildings and the proportional relations among various components. The dimensions of the framework of the top of the main hall and

■ Yellow glazed tile roofs of the Imperial Palace in Beijing.

the length of the beams decide the height of the roof, the size of the rooms and the length of rafters. The shape of the house, including the norm and size of the eaves and brackets, depend on the height of the pillars. The size and placement of the stylobates must also form proportionate relations with the height of the pillars. There are three types of steps inside and outside a building, called sloping, flat and gradual steps, built in accordance with practical needs.

As for colors, the formula was "blue in the east, white in the west, vermilion in the south, black in the north and yellow in the center".

This is also the reason why yellow glazed tiles were used only for palaces — indicating the location of central authority.

By the time when the Forbidden City was built, the rules for the construction of roofs had been defined. The hipped roof was considered the most supreme. Following in order were the gable and hip roof, overhanging gable roof, yingjian roof and zanjian roof.

Strict standards gradually emerged for the height, size, width and length, roof, color and decoration of buildings for people of different social strata. Usurping the style for one's superiors was a punishable offence.

■ The Hall of Heavenly Purity in the Forbidden City, serving as the sleeping quarter of the emperors of the Qing Dynasty.

Big Trees

The Chinese have always been fond of planting trees in their courtyards and around tombs. Because trees live longer than humans, they are regarded as symbols of longevity, and so the Chinese people have an affinity for them both in life and in death.

The Confucius Woods, where China's most influential thinker and educator Confucius is buried, in Qufu, Shandong Province, covers more than two million square meters. According to the *Commentary on the Waterways* by Li Daoyuan, "After Confucius died, his disciples planted exotic trees from different parts of the land around his grave. That is why there

■ The Confucius Woods.

are so many exotic trees which the later generations in the State of Lu could not name." In the Confucius Woods, there is a pistachio tree said to have been planted by Zi Gong, Confucius' leading disciple, personally. It was struck by lightening in later times, but its remains are still visible. Sticks made from other pistachio trees, the ruyi (S-shaped wand symbolic of good luck) and the alpine yarrow are called the "three treasures of the Confucius Woods".

In the grounds of the Confucius Family Mansion, there are some famous trees. There used to be three Chinese junipers said to have been planted by Confucius himself at the Dacheng Gate, but two of them were destroyed in 1214. In addition, a Chinese scholartree was planted in the Tang Dynasty and two ginkgo trees in the Song Dynasty in the courtyard of the Hall of Literary Scholars.

The cypress is a tree attracting special veneration in China. In the Xuanyuan Temple in Huangling County, Shaanxi Province, there are more than 60,000 ancient cypresses. Legend has it that a cypress standing at the entrance to the temple was planted by the Yellow Emperor. It is more than 19 meters tall and has a circumference of more than 10 meters. Another cypress, located by the western steps of the main hall, is called the "armor cypress", because Emperor Wu of the Han Dynasty is said to have once hung his armor on it.

The Yuanling Tomb of Liu Xiu, Emperor Guangwu of Eastern Han, is located at Mengjin, Henan Province, on the southern bank of the Yellow River. The emperor, well known for thrift and frugality, ordered that his tomb be a plain one, with no valuable funeral objects. There are 1,500 cypresses around his tomb, which were planted in the later Sui and Tang dynasties. In addition, there are 28 cypresses lining the path leading to the main hall of the tomb, which symbolize the 28 generals who assisted him in winning the throne.

In Sichuan, southwest China, there is a "road of royal cypresses". These are the descendents of cypresses planted to mark the progress of an obscure mountain path by General Zhang Fei of the Kingdom of Shu (221-263) during the Three Kingdoms period. There are now more than 8,000 ancient cypresses along the road, connecting Guangyuan in the north with Langzhong in the southeast.

■ Cypresses around the Mausoleum of the Yellow Emperor.

Chapter **5**

Memories of Quadrangular Residential Compounds

Quadrangular Residential Compounds and Hutong

Big as the city of Beijing is and small as a house is, they are both quadrangular residential compounds. This is the most unique characteristic of traditional Chinese structures.

The quadrangular residential compounds (siheyuan) are most commonly seen in north and northwest China, but those in Beijing are the most famous. The exquisite horizontal inscribed boards, verandas, screens, latticed windows and flowery gates are all saturated with the empathy of the wood they are made from and the scent of the cooked food of the human world.

The layout of the city of Beijing in

■ Quadrangular residential compound (siheyuan), Beijing.

■ Ya'er Hutong, Beijing.

some aspects even today preserves the tradition of the Yuan Dynasty capital Dadu. For example, some streets, architectural styles and the siheyuan are legacies of that dynasty ruled by Mongolians. The siheyuan and the narrow alleys, known as hutong, grew together to become representatives of the traditional culture and folk customs of Beijing.

The siheyuan became the main form of residential housing in the northern part of China. Because the climate, building materials and cultural tradition were similar in this region, the form and structure of the siheyuan are basically the same. However, the siheyuan of the Qiao family of Shanxi Province is unusually large. Moreover, on the Loess Plateau the siheyuan are formed of cave dwellings, and in northeast China several siheyuan occupied by different families can form a unit.

The siheyuan is based on the idea of enclosure. Generally speaking, just inside the front gate is a screen wall which blocks the line of vision from outside. There are almost no windows open to the outside. Therefore, once the front gate is closed, the compound is isolated from the outside world. Its inside becomes a small society in which there is respect for the seniors, and the seniors and juniors are differentiated. The people inside live a carefree life as a small family, and stand aloof from worldly affairs. People seem to be pieces of furniture surrounded by wood. Some people sit by a carved and painted table for a whole day, and the old-fashioned wooden armchair might be a family heirloom passed down for generations.

Under the Same Roof

Traditionally, the Chinese favored indoor activities, not like Westerners who traveled worldwide. There were many reasons. "When the parents are alive, do not travel far" was one of the reasons. More important, of course, is the family, the life of the family and the available arts of retreating toward the innermost being, such as calligraphy, poems and painting.

The wooden houses and siheyuan stood with respect for each other. They did not vie with each other, and were not aggressive. What they strove for was always to achieve a kind of tacit understanding with Nature. Therefore, the biggest success was to keep their life harmonious and happy on this land, and keep it unchanged. This kind of tranquil life became

a constant of happiness. Yes, the Chinese people understand their ordinary happiness like this at most times, and
what they want now is nothing more than to avoid degeneration.

The Chinese living in compounds are good at distributing
or enjoying the fun and pleasure from the limited materials in
the world of one family living in one house, and even in the
decoration and beautification of every detail of the small
family life. In the world, only the Chinese could paint pictures
of grotesque rocks, with the meter and rhyme of the simplicity
and plainness of the natural form retained, which was the
acme of beauty in the eyes of the Chinese. Also because of
the cultivation of the internal life, the heart of the Chinese

■ The Hall of Mental
Cultivation in the For-
bidden City, Beijing.

■ The Yuyuan Garden in Shanghai.

always grows together with the growth of the forelegs of a grasshopper, the feet of a centipede, the wings of a dragonfly, or a blade of grass. Therefore, they tend to be meticulous. They could almost explore the substance of beauty from a tiny piece of grit or a pebble, and they have always explored it like this — to get the last moment of joy from this miserable world with excitement. Even if war should break out, they could still be fascinated to see a cat approach a rat slowly.

The life of retreating to the innermost being was no doubt the safest, because it could give pleasure at any time, almost without any conditions. Therefore, it gradually became the most important inner being of the Chinese people, and the scholar-officials and literati in particular. They were so addicted to this kind of life that they repeatedly expressed its joys in poems, paintings and calligraphic works. Wang Anyi once said when speaking of the Yuyuan Garden, "It is a good idea for people to see the exquisite and the small. Here is an enchanting place of beauty seen through the eye of a needle. Hills multiply and streams double back, seeming to serve as a cover-up; rocks and pebbles are piled up as tall buildings, rising into the clouds; and paths crisscross as if the mountains were high and the roads were long. All this is intended to show ingenuity and cleverness."

Patriarchal Clan Rules and the Clan System

The siheyuan was occupied by one household as a unit. It had a salient feature: The people who lived inside did not visit each other. When the siheyuan clustered together they formed a hutong, and the hutong became a basic "social unit" and the public place where the people from the compounds could interact. It was also an important place for protecting the "social character" of the people. However, everything was determined inside the compound, and the people could not have many "exchanges" in the relatively public zone, because the compound was exactly the place where they settled down in their lives and careers. Whatever they talked about outside, they returned to their old selves when back home.

Essentially, the closed character of the hutong culture was only an extension of the siheyuan. There was no space for individuality. Everything had to fit in with etiquette, social status and rules. Therefore, etiquette gradually became a fixed pattern, a routine. Hypocrisy invaded the character of the people in the hutong bit by bit. Jean-Paul Sartre wrote, "An individual must try to be different from others, to be aloof from the philistine, and show uniqueness in all matters. This is the only thing not detrimental to self-value. Otherwise, if an individual is sunk into the collective and the masses, doing nothing and muddling on without any clear objective in life, he or she will lose too much personality, and the value of a human being." This may be true in other countries, but it was not true in traditional China. Even today, it is not yet universally understood how important the life of the individual is. Lu Xun said, "The Chinese have always been self-important — unfortunately, not as individuals. They are all patriotically self-important in groups. This is why they cannot extricate themselves and brace up after losing the cultural competition. This is the peculiar people who declare war on the mediocre while the latter is the mediocre who declare war on the minority of the talented." Individuality can always grow bit by bit in the modern system obtained from the new "cultural competition".

The people in the hutong are all automatically divided into groups. Of course, some of the groups are close and others are distant. If they walk to and fro only in the hutong, the relations between man and man include mainly relations by

■ The ancestral temple of the Yu family in Wuyuan County, Jiangxi Province.

■ Front columns of the Hall of the Goddess in the Jinci Temple, Shanxi Province, with carved wooden dragons, Song Dynasty.

blood and inter-personal relations by hutong. If the hutong is homologous to the patriarchal clan system, the smallest social inter-personal relations of the hutong is homologous to the "orientation by sense of shame" with stress on authority. The feudal patriarchal clan relations were precisely the fundamental cause for the backwardness of Chinese society, because they made the people unable to unite to resist humiliation from outside.

Retrogressing Individuals

Sticks and canes were used by teachers in traditional schools to discipline the students. This is based on the concept of eliminating the independent self just discussed above. The story goes that one day Han Shan asked Shi De, "If someone insults me, humiliates me, cold-shoulders me,

■ Old theatrical stage, Qing Dynasty.

■ The yamen (government office) of Pingyao County, Shanxi Province.

laughs at me, looks down on me, slanders me, hurts me, dislikes me, hates me, cheats me, and deceives me, what should I do?" Shi De replied, "Just put up with it. Obey him, give in, respect him, get away from him, tolerate him with patience, pretend to be deaf and dumb, don't say a word, and watch with a cold eye. Wait and see how he ends up."

This is by no means a joke. Tolerance is a respected art of self-restraint. Proceeding from the patriarchal clan system, after being wrapped in traditional ethnics and feudal etiquette, the character of the Chinese could only follow the advice of people like She De. Lin Yutang once summed this up, saying, "The skilful realization of the life and the natural instinct of mankind have always constituted the ideal of the Chinese moral character. And from this realization have derived other good virtues, such as peace, being content with one's lot, calmness and tolerance. These are the distinct characteristics of the Chinese moral character."

From this we can enumerate the characteristics of the Chinese national moral character: 1. firmness, 2. purity and simplicity, 3. love for Nature, 4. tolerance, 5. doing what one likes, 6. wittiness, 7. high reproductive rate, 8. diligence, 9. frugality, 10. love for family life, 11. moderation, 12. being content with one's lot, 13. humor, 14. conservativeness, and 15. love for woman's beauty.

The Chinese nation has been destined to be known to the world for the characteristics of its group-oriented culture. It has continued and developed the national group culture characterized by external influences and mutual support and dependence. It is different from the Western culture, with individualism and self-support as its main characteristics. This perhaps can also be seen as the main reason why other old civilizations with similarly long histories became extinct before the advent of modern industrial civilization while Chinese civilization endured, and can release its new vigor and vitality today when industrial civilization is highly developed. Take the life of the people living in a traditional siheyuan for example. Born in an environment surrounded by houses on all sides, he or she grew up with Chinese toon or bamboo and trees in the yard, aged with the beams and pillars in the house, and was placed in a wooden coffin in the main hall after death, with a memorial tablet left behind. Finally, he or she was moved to the graveyard for eternal rest with the memorial tablet placed in the ancestral temple. This cycle was repeated from generation to generation, and time buries everything and keeps giving birth to visible hope.

■ Female statue, Western Han Dynasty, unearthed at Mawangdui, Changsha, Hunan Province.

Chapter **6**

The Mean in the Wood

Doctrine of the Mean

In Chinese teahouses, on a fan, on a screen and even on a tea cup, we can often see the four characters "难得糊涂" (it's folly to be wise).

Zheng Banqiao's free-style handwriting brought rare naturalness and freedom to the spirit of the Chinese. Of course, it is also an art of life. An American missionary named Arthur Henderson Smith (1845-1932) wrote in his book *Chinese Characteristics* that a thing like poverty has become an art in the hands of the Chinese. The art of poverty has its positive and negative aspects. The positive aspect is diligence and the negative aspect is thrift. And both diligence and thrift depend on patience. A man without patience cannot be industrious and thrifty. The Chinese possess all the three characteristics. The three of them can cooperate fully with each other, and the harder the life, the more unbreakable their relations of cooperation.

Another book by a foreign author in the 19th century also wrote of the hardships of the Chinese, "To us, the primary thing is their characteristics of competing in the world labor market. They are good farmers, good mechanics, good laborers, and good sailors. They have wisdom, correct feelers, and the untiring patience needed for becoming first-rate machinists and manufacturers, in addition to their virtues of submissiveness, honesty, plainness, hard work, self-denial and tolerance, their love for peace and their ability to bear the bad weather of both winter and summer. If they are given the necessary education and guidance, in addition to capital and enterprises, they will become the best workers in the world. The experience in the United States, Australia, India and Southeast Asia is sufficient to show this."

Chinese culture stresses the character "中", and many Chinese characters such as 中、束、柬 are distinct representations of the central axis line. It can be well said that traditional Chinese culture was full of gates which led everywhere. But sometimes, there were some shortcuts. If the "gate of vitality" was found, it led to all places.

■ Old residential houses
in southern Anhui Province.

The Story of Wood

Everything wanted to be in the center, or to have the central place reserved for it. The result was that, ideologically, it disliked all excessive theory and, morally, it disliked all excessive behavior. This was what Lin Yutang said. He himself had a deep knowledge of the doctrine of the mean. Therefore, he knew the position of the doctrine of the mean in the hearts of the Chinese. He even inferred that the term "China" was not only a physiographic generalization, but also a milestone in man's journey in life. The golden mean is, in substance, the normal course conforming to human nature. Ancient scholars followed the doctrine of the mean, boasting that they had discovered the most fundamental principle of philosophy and saying that average or middling (中) was the correct path of the world, and mediocre "庸" was the theorem of the world. Returning to the original words of Confucius, this is, "The moral character of a gentle man may be supreme!"

The best example of the process from the mean to conciliation, following the public, upholding justice and fairness, tactfulness and ingenuity is provided by the board game weiqi (go), the pieces and board for which are made of wood. Weiqi is originally full of fighting and strangling. It is a kind of competition for blank spaces and seizing ground, it is seizure, pressing and encirclement, and a game of life and death for either the black or the white. However, in the eyes of Master Wu Qingyuan, "The highest realm of weiqi is harmony rather than competition, winning or losing."

It is better to have no tricks than to have tricks. Giving no thought to winning or losing and keeping only harmony in the heart coincides with the original intention of weiqi. If it was created by a sage, it must have been his hope to attain harmony by making use of the black and white world. This is why a player of a higher duan (class) will often make a winning or losing move or a wrong move at an appropriate time, because what he is seeking is the mean of harmony in the whole game.

Happiness of the Rational

Man proposes, God disposes. It seems that after living long in a wooden house, man would gradually become accustomed to the nature of wood, become natural and elegant, and stand aloof from worldly affairs. However, standing aloof from worldly affairs cannot constitute natural behavior. Therefore, there must be a more profound life philosophy that plays a role in their minds. This is tolerance evolved from the mean.

One who can endure is safer. A man is of high moral character when he asks for no help from others, be always reserved in speech, remains aloof from things of no immediate concern to oneself, and be careful lest extreme joy beget sorrow. Water flowing out in a trickle takes a long time to run dry. There are many other maxims like these. They are all natural criteria observed by the Chinese in handling world affairs.

Wooden houses and utensils alone could not provide sufficient scope for man's ever-expanding activities. Therefore, proper expansion had to give people more leisure and a richer life through greater garden space. The gardens thus became

■ Zither recital.

part of the home life of the Chinese, and the Chinese liked such a life from the very beginning.

The symbolism of the garden also lies in the fact that it is the external condition for cooperation between man and society, and with which it prompts and protects human souls from clashing with the external surroundings. A gentleman does not go against things, nor offend anyone or anything. A bigger space always belongs to the self. Relaxation of the mood brings further artistic space. Relaxation often depends on "the cultivation of mental tranquility". Don't go to extremes in anything you do or say. Leave some room for maneuver. Don't eat too much, nor work too hard. It is necessary to fully appreciate the group character of the Chinese. *Tending the Roots of Wisdom* is a very good book. It is a guide to the philosophy of life based on practical experiences of getting along with others.

A similar book is *Sword Play in Zuigu Hall*. It purports to teach people how to behave in society. Its dictum "it's a remote mountain when you close the doors, and it's the Pure Land everywhere when you read" is often quoted and observed. It advocates shutting oneself in the house and retreating into one's innermost being. Even an elegant and leisurely life should be aimed at "gratifying oneself" and "finding satisfaction". One should not miss any chance to "cultivate mental tranquility". Moreover, the Shaolin Temple, the Moji paintings, *Zuo's Chronicles*, Sima Qian's *Historical Records*, Xue Tao's letters, You Jun's notes, Nanhua sutras, Xiangru's prose works and Qu Yuan's long poem *Encountering Sorrow* are all superb works of art that guide people into the history of the past and the present, and can integrate the mind with Heaven and Nature.

If two words must be used to generalize the negative factors of Chinese culture, they are etiquette and reason (or logic). Concealment, deception, lies and devouring humans as criticized by Lu Xun spread unchecked under this mechanism. Of course, Confucian orthodoxy also helped suppress people's wisdom in all aspects. As a result, nobody tried to seek clear thoughts. Finally, they could only, bit by bit, escape to seek the visible happiness of the rational and idle away their lives. Therefore, a very tiny thing could be enlarged into joy. The process itself was a great joy. Physical laborers did not need science. And if a man had no chance to stand aloof from the yellowed ancient books, it would be better not to have intelligence, because that would disturb the mind. This often caused people great distress. It also led people to seek more material pursuits. The Taoists believed from the very beginning that material wealth could only bring confusion to people's minds.

Chinese Buddhism

Democracy and science were closely related to man's work of discovery and cultivation. The important contribution made by the Renaissance to civilization was the discovery of man. Man was raised to the height of being juxtaposed with Heaven and Earth in Chinese culture, but why was individual character suppressed in so many ways?

There is no identical view on this either in Taoism, Confucianism or Buddhism. They all laid stress on the "mind". The "mind" was also designed beforehand. Some people said that "my mind means realization", others said that only when "I" was forgotten in the "mind" (or heart) coul it be true "freedom from worry" and that one could wake up to reality. Neo-Confucianism once issued "A Proclamation to the World's Peoples on Chinese Culture", saying, "The first point that the Westerners should learn from the Oriental culture, is the spirit of 'the present being right' and the concept of 'putting down everything'." Traditional Chinese culture regarded disposition as the root source of all values. Therefore, when man was conscious of his disposition, the value of life and the value of the universe were both present. The life of a man was immediately placed in instant thinking. This is exactly the so-called realm of life in which "we have no other request, and the present is right". The gist of that passage is "sincere allegiance", and is basically what Zhang Zai (1020-1077) once said, "Make up your mind for Heaven

■ Wooden niches for Buddhist statues in the main hall
of the Jingtu Temple, Yingxian County, Shanxi Province.

and Earth, establish your Heaven-ordained being for the
people, carry on the unique and matchless learning of the
sages, and preserve peace for all generations."

"Make up your mind" was the highest pursuit of man. The
highest realm of the mind was to go up to Heaven and down
into the Earth, and travel through the boundless universe
without any limits. But what actual use was this to the ordinary
person? Perhaps, just because these things were too "fine",
they were obstacles to attaining the innate nature and original
intention of a person.

Everyone wanted to be a good man, and everyone wanted
to practice austerities to remove the obstacles from the mind.

The Story of Wood

Xunzi's theory of inborn evil, instead of alerting the people, increased their determination to make further efforts to practice austerities. When Buddhism was first introduced into China, it found a way to convince the people to believe in it, by preaching that "all living beings have the Buddha nature". During the Northern and Southern Dynasties, Master Dao'an said that everyone could become a Buddha through the cultivation of one's moral character. As long as one kept on cultivating one's moral character, one would become a Buddha, whether in the present life or in the next life. Therefore, more and more people came to believe in Buddhism. This was, of course, a great help to society, and of great good to each individual. After all, to believe in Buddhism was, in the final analysis, to believe in one's own mind, or "primary force", because the "mind", which the ordinary people had no time to know, sprang from the great "mind" of traditional culture. Chinese Buddhism and even the basic character of some of the Chinese people were thus developed.

When you have a good understanding of this formidable "mind", you may understand a large part of Chinese culture. This mind is not only a simple tool, it is also a methodology. Only when you grasp it, can you seek other pursuits, pass in and out freely, and open "two doors, or even three or four doors, from one mind".

The sudden or gradual awakening to the truth in Buddhism both refer to the "mind". Exercising self-restraint and returning to propriety as advocated by the Confucian and the Taoist ideal of removing all desires were all intended to help people calm their minds. It is perhaps not too much of an exaggeration to say that the main body of traditional Chinese culture is the mind.

Wang Shouren (1472-1529), a philosopher of the Ming Dynasty, was a disciple of Cheng Hao (1032-1085) and Zhu Xi (1130-1200), philosophers of the Song Dynasty. In order to practice Zhu Xi's teachings, he once made up his mind to investigate the principles of the bamboo. For seven days and seven nights he thought only of bamboo, but he reached no enlightenment. He was so exhausted that he fell ill. However, he never gave up his mental striving. Later, exiled to a mountainous area in southwest China, he suddenly became aware of the central idea of the *Great Learning*, one of the Confucian classics. He then re-interpreted the classic on the basis of his own understanding, thereby becoming a great master of "intuitive learning".

■ The Temple of Heaven, Beijing.

Buddhism flourished in the Wei, Jin, and Northern and Southern Dynasties. Taoism also made great progress. Buddhist and Taoist temples were built one after another. Many Buddhist followers offered their houses as Buddhist temples. Aristocrats and bureaucrats did the same. Buddhist temples were built not only in the cities and suburbs, but also in places with beautiful surroundings.

The Taoist Spirit

In ancient times, the Legalists stressed positive experiences in life, the Taoists advocated limited renunciation of worldly affairs, and the Confucians gave proper consideration to the balance between the subject and object of life. In the cultural genes of the Chinese people, the process of limited entry into society was accompanied by a positive and easy life at a proper pace, so that the culture always had propulsion.

It was very easy for Confucianism and Taoism to blend with each other. Because of the easy blending, the Chinese were eager to outdo others when they were young, but after they were in their 30s, they gradually became calm and moderate. On the one hand, you are eager to make progress, but on the other, the law of the movement and development of things always changes in the opposite direction. Laozi, the founder of Taoism, said, "Opposites are complementary." Therefore, you don't have to pay too much attention to the present, and there's no need to mind temporary troubles.

What belongs to you will surely come to you, but you will not get what you should not get no matter how hard you try. Most Chinese believe this.

Confucius, who founded the Confucian school, also adopted some Taoist ideas. Legend has it that he once asked Laozi for advice about Taoism. Another story goes that one day Confucius visited Mount Tai, where he met a cheerful man who was singing and playing a zither. He asked the man why he was so happy. The latter answered, "Heaven has

■ The Doulao Hall of the Taoist Qingyang Temple in Chengdu, Sichuan Province.

given birth to all things, and man is the most precious thing. As I am a man, I am happy. This is the first reason. There are differences between men and women, and man is respected. As I am a man, I am happy. This is my second reason. There are people who cannot see anything after they are born, but I am in my 70s, so I am happy. This is my third reason. Scholars are always poor, and death is the end of one's life. Since I am poor and am waiting for the end of my life, why should I not be happy?"

You don't have to make great efforts to attain a worldly objective; depend on your mind, and your mind will be free. The strength of the mind is great. Why don't you use this function of your mind? Is happiness not feeling? Feeling can be achieved through the mind.

In a sense, Confucianism, Taoism and Buddhism are not genuine religions, but they have often played the role of quasi-religion. For example, the Confucian doctrine of worshipping Heaven and showing pity for others awed people. They often made self-introspections, and had a sober understanding of their own limitations. The doctrine "do not unto others as you would not have them do unto you" can be seen as an everyday rule for the maintenance of person-to-person relations. However, this must be placed among the other rules in modern society for "re-exchange", so that it can better perform its traditional function of inertia on the basis of awakening the subjective consciousness and personal dignity of the people.

Chapter **7**

The Corbel Bracket
as an Example

Oriental Structure

Under the 人-shaped Chinese roof is the truss. How the truss is laid out affects the projecting eaves and, of course, the internal space rhythm and man's overall experience inside. The things inside and outside are connected with each other, and form a complicated but orderly group, constituting the aesthetics of the Oriental structure.

It's very easy to define the structure of Chinese-style houses. Generally speaking, there are three styles: the strutted purlin roof truss, column-and-tie structure, and clay-wood structure.

■ The Guanyin Pavilion at the Dule Temple, Tianjin.

The strutted purlin roof truss means that there is more than one beam. Generally speaking, a beam is placed on the columns, and a number of short posts are erected on the beam. Another beam is placed on the short posts. Some structures have two tiers of beams, while in others, the beams and purlins are placed tier upon tier until they reach the top of the roof. Then a ridge post is used to bear the ridge purlin, to form a multi-tier wood framework. In this construction, the beams are equal to a series of steps forming a support with a clear logic and compact structure. Standing in the house, you have to look up to see them. When your eyes are fixed on the vertical and horizontal wooden members, you may think that you are in a labyrinth.

Supported by vertical posts and columns, the beams have formed one space after another from generation to generation. The enclosure and separation of the spaces freely expresses the mood of the builders.

The characteristics of the column-and-tie structure are: A number of columns are erected along the depth of a house equal to the number of purlins, on which the rafters are arranged in order. The load of the roof is passed directly to the columns through the purlins, without using beams. The rows of columns are connected by the tie-beams, which are pierced through the columns to form a roof truss. Ties are used to connect every two roof trusses to form the space framework of a room. In order to save wood, shorter columns are erected on the tie-beams between every two ground columns, and the number of tiers of column-bearing tie-beams is increased as a result. The tie-beams become outrigger beams after piercing through the eave columns to

bear and support the overhanging eaves. Therefore, the tie-beams also perform part of the function of the outrigger beams. In this type of construction, the rafters are directly nailed to the purlins, and tiles are laid on the rafters. The whole roof is made lighter to promote its quake resistance.

Chinese-style buildings use earth and wood as basic materials. According to the theory of yin and yang and that of the "five elements", earth is at the center of all things, and therefore earth must be used in order to ensure stability and order to the building.

■ The Jingzhen Octagonal Pavilion with a wooden roof in Menghai, Yunnan Province, built in 1701.

The Main Beam

The main beam is also called the transverse beam. It refers to the principal transverse wooden member supported on the round wood columns to form the ridge. In general, pinewood, elm wood and Chinese fir with good texture are used for the purpose. The cross beam is one of the principal members of traditional Chinese wood construction. A building depends on the main beam to bear its weight. Moreover, in consideration of the visual effect, the length of the main beam is not much different from the height between the beam and the ground.

The main beam carries the upper half of the whole construction. It and the other wooden members above it form the frame. There are two types of frames: the supporting beam type and the column-and-tie type.

In the Chinese folk tradition, there are various ceremonies postulated for the placing of the main beam. Since it is the final stage of the main work for a building, the ceremony marks a very solemn and sensitive festivity. It is solemn, because a new building is about to be completed; it is sensitive because there is always a worry that some unexpected problem might crop up, which would be considered an ill omen. On the appointed day, firecrackers would be exploded and eight able-bodied young men would carry the main beam, wrapped in a sheet of red paper, on their shoulders. The guest of honor would unwrap the red paper to reveal the Chinese character "福" (happiness, or good luck) painted in the very center of the beam. This is called "receiving good luck". Then, the young men mount ladders in time with the directions of the head carpenter, and lay the beam in its place. The head carpenter climbs onto the beam, and throws steamed buns, cakes and sweets down to the assembled crowd below. This is called "distributing the good luck". He chants the words "good luck for the laying of the beam" and "the lucky star shines high above" while he does so. The crowd scrambles for the gifts, in order to "have the luck". The head carpenter sings a special song for the occasion at the top of his voice. While he sings, the crowd responds with "hai". Finally, red paper posters with the Chinese characters "紫气东来" (the auspicious purple essence comes from the east), and "太公在此，百无禁忌"(when Patriarch Jiang is present, all taboos are in abeyance) are pasted on the beam. The head carpenter steps down, and the host offers his close relatives and friends a feast.

Sometimes, a talisman would be placed on the beam to repel evil spirits. Other crucial wooden

■ Corbels supporting a wooden roof.

members, such as the angle purlins, might have coins, colored stones or other "warders-off of evil" placed on them. Such items have been found during the renovation of some buildings in the Summer Palace.

The Baoguo Temple in Ningbo, built in the sixth year (1014) of the Dazhong Xiangfu reign period of the Song Dynasty, is the oldest wooden building extant in southern China. Uniquely designed, the structure has no beams, despite the fact that the main hall has a width of 11.91 meters and a depth of 13.91 meters.

Dismembering of Corbel Bracket

Unlike the monotony and independence of Greek columnar architecture, traditional Chinese architecture relies on the corbel bracket to link the roof, columns and column bases to form a natural integrity.

There are three versions about the origin of the corbel bracket. One theory is that it evolved from the projecting parts of the intersections of log cabin construction. Another theory is that it evolved from the outrigger beams that pierced the columns. The third theory is that it evolved from the brace or the trimmer beam of the eave-supporting column.

During the Western Zhou Dynasty (1046-771 BC), big trapezoidal bearing blocks were used to support heavy bronze sacrificial vessels. During the Han Dynasty (206 BC-220 AD), large numbers of corbel brackets began to appear on stone pillars erected in front of temples and tombs. The image can

■ Elaborate corbel.

also be seen on burial objects, as well as stone and brick relief carvings of the same period. Corbel brackets were used on pillars in the subsequent dynasties. At first, the corbel bracket was in the shape of the Chinese character "人" (man), i.e., a forking support with a block placed above on the architrave to bear the eave purlins. From the Tang Dynasty to the Yuan Dynasty, the principal characteristic of the corbel bracket was that the beam supported by the pillar corbel bracket was inserted in the corbel bracket in most cases, so that the latter and the beam frame were tightly joined together, and the bracket overhanging from the building also joined the column-top lintel. The column-top lintels around the building and the front and side beams that formed right angles with the lintels were interlinked to form a horizontal frame separated into several square lattices, and the corbel brackets became the strengthened joints at the intersections. As it was an "intersecting member", it could also be regarded as a part of the horizontal frame.

According to the *Rules of Architecture* of the Song Dynasty, as the corbel brackets of the frames were joined to the beams in all halls, the bearing function of the corbel brackets was reduced. In the book, each unit of the corbel bracket was called a duo. The corbel bracket on the column was called zhutou puzuo (column-top bracket), that on the corner pillar was called zhuanjiao puzuo (corner bracket), and that on the column-top tie between two columns was called bujian puzuo (intermediate bracket). There was a dadou (larger block) at the bottom of each duo, holding up the whole bracketing unit, also called ludou (capital block). A cross was opened on the capital block, and two bracket units, one vertical and one horizontal, were placed on the cross. The vertical unit was called huagong (projecting bracket), and the horizontal one was called nidao gong (nidao bracket). Each layer overhanging from the corbel bracket was a tiao (step), and each layer added was a pu (bracket). The *Overall Bracketing Order of the Rules of Architecture* states, "One step projected is called four puzuo (brackets), two steps projected is called five brackets, three steps projected is called six brackets, four steps projected is called seven brackets, and five steps projected is called eight brackets." The size and grade of the corbel bracket system were determined by the number of steps projected and the number of brackets.

During the Ming Dynasty, big and small efang (architraves) and suiliang fang (architraves along the beam) were used between two pillar tops, and the size of the corbel bracket was reduced once again, the spacing increased and the decoration emphasized. Each corbel bracket unit in the

Qing Dynasty was called one zan. wangong was used on each guagong (shortest inner or outer bracket). The guagong and wangong were called zhengxin or right-in-the-middle (or center), inner and outer, depending on their positions. For example, the wangong on the right-in-the-middle guagong was called right-in-the-middle wangong, those in front of the corbel bracket were called outer guagong and outer wangong, and those behind the corbel bracket were called inner guagong and inner wangong. Another kind of corbel bracket in the Qing Dynasty, called the "gold-plated corbel bracket", was used for the pingshenke under the outer eaves or double eaves. In the front was an ang (slanting arm) and at the tail was a yibujia beam slanting upward.

Corbel bracket was reduced to a mere decorative member during the Qing Dynasty.

The history of the evolution of dougong (corbel bracket) indicates that it was first placed only on the column or the outer end of the outrigger beam to convey the load of the beam and bear the weight of the eaves to increase the depth of the protruding eaves. It is precisely because of this that foreign architects say that the greatest contribution of ancient China to architecture was the corbel bracket.

Chapter 8

The Arc of the East

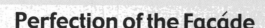

Perfection of the Facáde

Oriental architecture stressed the accumulation of energy and the cultivation of moral character. Apart from the columns or pillars, the walls, enclosure walls and screen walls were all a kind of natural restraint. You may feel that these auxiliary facilities are somewhat closed or conservative, but don't forget there are doors and windows as links with the mind and soul.

China is a country that stresses facádes. There are many kinds of doors in traditional Chinese architecture: guangliang door or gate, ruyi door or gate, mantou gate, wuji gate, pailou gate, hua gate, suiqiang gate, yuedong gate, and so on. The shape, structure, character, fengshui (geomancy) status, position, color and taboos of gates and doors constitute the complicated culture of these communication spaces.

In addition to the doors, there are complicated and versatile windows. They open to the outside for light and ventilation, but are used to partition the internal space, and to extend, replace or reflect all kinds of scenes and views. Windows, like a moving picture frame, keep changing the inner angles and face the sky, cloud shadows and the weather of all seasons, showing exchanges between Heaven and Earth. Windows are always likened to bright, flickering eyes. Moreover, each

■ The Long Corridor in the
Summer Palace, Beijing.

building has its own unique window designs.

The Chinese for railing is langan. The vertical wood is called the post (lan), and the horizontal wood is called the rail (gan). Railings have the connotation of being romantic places in Chinese folklore. They were often placed high in a building for lonely ladies to await heart-breaking stories.

The ceiling is called tianhua (heavenly flowers). It was thought that immortals resided there. A caisson ceiling is called zaojing. The character jing means a water well. Because wood is highly inflammable, it was thought that calling the ceiling a well would dampen it.

There are many paintings, carvings and handicraft articles in the house of a traditional scholar-official. The rooms feature white walls, black frames, dark-brown furniture and painted table screens. On most of these wooden articles are depictions of birds and beasts, plants and flowers, as well as inscribed poems, naturally and perfectly forming a place full of Chinese flavor.

Man as an Integral Part of Nature

The ancient Chinese culture was multiple and composite. Its main body, the Huaxia culture, is based in the north and the south geographically, branching out from the Yellow River and the Yangtze River respectively. The north was symbolized by the dragon, and the south by the phoenix. As to the main schools of thought, Confucianism dominated the north, and Taoism dominated the south. The Huaxia culture during

■ Wooden screen, Qing Dynasty.

the Spring and Autumn and Warring States periods was represented by the State of Jin in the north, and the State of Chu in the south. Psychologically, people are divided into four categories: the enthusiastic, the emotional, the cold and the sentimental. It so happened that the first two characteristics coincided with Confucianism, while the latter two were characteristics of the southerners.

Architecture reflected this dualism. Ancient architecture roughly developed from cave dwellings in the north and hut dwellings in the south to multiple types of dwellings. The main topic of our discussion is on the theme "man as an integral part of Nature" in the Huaxia culture.

Take the culture of the State of Chu for example. The Chinese philosophy then was centered on the relationship between Nature and Man. The people of the State of Chu believed that individuals were driven by the desire to transcend Nature. Therefore, exterior things should coincide with the innermost being of the individual. The natural existence of man was limited, but man could enter into the infinite in time and space by transcending Nature. Man must demand more than what existed in nature. Therefore, man must have men-

■ A mural at the Dunhuang Mogao Grottoes.

tal existence and pursuits so that he would not lose his objective and himself. In the philosophy of the Chu people, man was an individual who could consciously integrate himself with the universe. As long as he lived, man could consciously integrate himself with Nature, and eventually reach the infinite. Life was even more practical and profound when it had something to attach itself to and had a higher pursuit. With the spirit in which man was an integral part of Nature, man could free himself from all limitations, and release his whole energy. The "perfect man", "divine man", "sage" and "true man" mentioned in *Zhuangzi* were all conscious pursuits of man.

Becoming an integral part of Nature was the highest pursuit, and all aspects of life were involved. In arts, people sought central harmony, plainness, restraint and implicitness. This was equally true of architecture. This characteristic was distinct in the buildings of the State of Chu. With the main part built of wood, the buildings feature the integration of restrained and reserved natural beauty, lightness, firmness, affinity and simplicity. The structures were inlaid in Nature, making the people living in them an organic part of Nature.

The horizontal layers of the eaves and the corridors and railings on different levels of Chu structures all look at the earth as if they have deep affection for it. The roofs, ridges and curves look like the lines which can be found everywhere on the earth. The Chinese at that time did not have the God of the Christianity, but they had a longing and reverence for Nature, and were concerned with the fate of Heaven and Man. Wu Zixu of the State of Wu designed and built Wu's capital city of Helu (the Chengxiang District of Suzhou City today). "Zixu studied the soil and water, offered sacrifices to Heaven and Earth, and built a big city with a circumference of 47 *li* (equivalent to 23.5 km). There were eight gates on the land, symbolic of the eight gates to Heaven, and eight gates on the water, symbolic of the gates into the Earth. A smaller city was built with a circumference of 10 *li*, and three gates. There was no gate in the east so that there was no opening for the rival State of Yue. The front gate was kept open to symbolize the gate of Heaven open to the autumn winds. The Snake Gate was also kept open, to symbolize the door to the Earth." *(The Spring and Autumn Annals of Wu and Yue)*

Communication between Heaven and Man was often linked with the theory of the four deities, the theory of yin and yang and the theory of the five elements.

Man as an integral part of nature was a philosophy in itself. After it was combined with the rules of etiquette and the patriarchal clan system, it produced various kinds of rules and helped strengthen the original social system, and also led to the emergence of more types, shapes and structures in ancient architecture, such as ceremonial structures like terrace, altar, Buddhist temple, Taoist temple and park.

■ Wooden house of the Zhuang people in Jinzhuzhai, Guangxi Zhuang Autonomous Region.

Primitive Forms of Worship

■ Qiangmu wood mask from Hongyuan County, Sichuan Province.

In remote antiquity, many tribes linked the Earth, women and birth together. For example, during the ceremony of offering sacrifices to the Earth, vessels used by women were among the oblations. And it was considered better for women who had given birth to harvest cereals, because, in this way, they would impart fertility to the soil. Each tribe had its own mythologies and totems. The integration of Heaven and Man began with Heaven. Because the brightest objects in sky are the sun and the moon, the God of the Sun and the God of the Moon were worshipped. The sun, shining over the land to promote the growth of all things, is the source of life and is naturally linked with reproduction. Many nationalities worldwide have linked sex and the sun as a unified source of life.

■ Wooden statue of the goddess Guanyin, Ming Dynasty.

Therefore, many gods are simultaneously the God of the Sun and the God of Reproduction.

In ancient China, homologous worship of the sun was worship of the earth. "The Father of Heaven" and "the Mother of Earth" gazed upon each other, and all kinds of mysterious ideas emerged one after another. For example, the Manchu people believed that the heaven, the earth and human society all had three levels each. The ancient Uygurs believed that the earth had seven levels, and that man lived on the highest level, the surface of the earth. The people of the Han ethnic group thought that earthquakes were caused by the movements of a huge turtle which dwelt at the center of the earth, whereas the Manchu people attributed the disasters to the grandmother-in-law of the catfish turning her body.

In China, the word "heaven" was used as a term for the emperor. It was unfathomable and awe-inspiring. It was a social estate, authority and law. It produced everything (including the dragon). Therefore, it was inviolable. Because there were too many things that transcended life experiences, the worship of the deities and the legends enhanced each other. There was an endless stream of strained interpretations and analogies to explain life and natural phenomena. This gradually led to the formation of a national habit of thinking, a traditional fixed pattern, and a practical set of patterns of etiquette. For example, the design of traditional door knockers was borrowed from depictions of the mythical taotie beast and the dragons found on the bronze ware of the Shang Dynasty; the lotus flower was symbolic of the vulva; the peony was symbolic of the female; and the bird of the male was symbolic of the reproductive organ. For another example, the picture of numerous children, the wish for the early birth of a boy and other symbols were all turned into forms of plants and animals in image or homophonically and were then applied to the details of architecture.

■ Wooden statue of the God of the Earth.

Graceful Curves

Straight lines are alien to traditional Chinese architecture. This is because aesthetics in the Chinese tradition dictated that, when building a house, it should not be like a wedge intruding into Nature, but a beautiful arc in the heart. Beginning from the ground, it was ready to join Nature by growing upward.

In Chinese-style houses, the roofs slope downward in arcs. The rules for determining the gradient and arcs were juzhe (folding the roof) or jujia (the pitch and curvature of the roof). Juzhe appears in the *Rules of Architecture* of the Song Dynasty, and jujia is used in the *Rules of Works* issued by the Ministry of Works in the Qing Dynasty. The structural forms of the sloping roofs include the roof with a single slope, the roof with two slopes, the roof with four slopes and the zanjian roof.

Wood is, of course, a product of Nature. But when it is softened in fire, shaved by the planer and painted, wood obtained from Nature becomes a superior product.

Because there are curves everywhere, it looks as if there is no need for definite thinking, and the houses also look as if they have become blurred into universal magical boxes. Many things inside these magical boxes are moving, and their motion is closely linked with the curves. Apart from the "overhanging eaves" peculiar to Chinese architecture, the light and lively flying motion could be seen everywhere — in the roofs of pavilions, terraces, towers, palaces and temples.

The drawing of this graceful curve started very early. It looked as if man used this curve as his bow to the earth right after he landed from the trees. During China's first period of imperial prosperity, the Han Dynasty, dances, acrobatics, paintings and carvings all appeared in a flying and dancing form. The designs of that time were often composed of clouds, lightning and dancing dragons. The carvings were also often based on fierce winged beasts (its variations being somewhat similar to Pablo Picasso's cubistic painting style). The imagination and copying of flight gradually resulted in the deformed apsaras (flying fairies). The period from the Han Dynasty to the Tang Dynasty was a rare golden corridor of explosive imagination in Chinese culture, fully showing the vigor of the advance of this nation.

Chapter **9**

Garden Aesthetics

Strolling in Garden

China is a country with well developed horticulture. The *Management of Gardens*, the *Records of Gardens in the Yangtze River Delta*, the *Classical Gardens of Suzhou* and other specialized books have influenced the management of gardens as an aesthetic pursuit from generation to generation. The terms about gardening are too numerous to be mentioned one by one, but let me give an overview.

Artistic terms: yijing (poetic imagery), xiangdi (geomancy), buju (layout), zaojing (scene building), jiejing (scene borrowing), diaosu (sculpture) and bianlian (horizontal inscribed boards and couplets).

Garden plants: peizhi (disposition), jixiang (seasonal appearance), caoping (lawn), huatan (flower bed), huayuan (flower border), zhili (bush hedge), panyuan (climbing plants) and gushu (ancient trees).

Installations: dimao (landform), jiashan (rockery), zhishi (rock placement), lishui (water course arrangement), bo'an (dock wall), penquan (fountain) and yuanlu (path).

Ornaments: yuanting (pavilion), dimao (landform), yuanlang (corridor), shuixie (waterside pavilion), yuanqiao (bridge), yuanqiang (wall), fang (boat), huajia (trellis) and xiaopin (accessories).

Following is a list of China's leading classical gardens: Banmu Yuan (Banmou Garden),Zhuozheng Yuan (Humble Administrator's Garden), Liu Yuan (Lingering Garden), Shizi Lin (Lion Forest Garden), Canglang Ting (Gentle Waves Pavilion), Wangshi Yuan (Garden of the Master of the Fishing Net), Huanxiu Shanzhuang (Mountain Villa in Elegant Surroundings), Yi Yuan (Garden of Pleasantness), Ou Yuan (Couple's Garden Retreat), Yi Pu (Garden of Cultivation), Yongcui Shanzhuang (Mountain Villa Embracing Emerald Green), Chang Yuan (Carefree Garden), Hu Yuan (Teapot Garden), Canli Yuan (Garden of Remnant Particles), Xi Yuan (West Garden), Shou Xihu (Slender West Lake), Ge Yuan (Geyuan Garden), Jixiao Shanzhuang (Jixiao Mountain Villa), Xiao Pangu (Lesser Winding Valley), Pianshi Shanfang (Mountain House of Slabstones), Zhan Yuan (Zhanyuan Garden), Jichang Yuan (Jichang Garden), Yu Yuan (Yuyuan Garden), Qinghui Yuan (Garden of Clear Light), Yuyin Shanfang (Mountain House of Lingering Shades), Ke Yuan (Keyuan Garden), Xi Tang (West Pond), Qunxing Caotang (Thatched Hut of Stars), Xinfan Donghu (Xinfan East Lake),

■ Painting of the Yuanmingyuan Imperial Garden by Tang Dai and Shen Yuan of the Qing Dynasty and Chongqing'an Huachi (Painting Pond of Chongqing Studio). If the Imperial Summer Resort, Beihai Park, Yuanmingyuan, Summer Palace and other imperial gardens are added, the list will be much longer.

The gardens recreate natural surroundings. Large and elegant gardens appeared only in the Han Dynasty, when material wealth was relatively concentrated. An example of these early gardens is the Imperial Forest Park (Shanglin Yuan). Private gardens began to flourish only in the Northern and Southern Dynasties (420-589). Scholars in banishment or retirement created their own little worlds in their gardens, where they whiled away the time writing poems or painting landscapes.

Because it was a place for personal feelings, the private gardens, built according to the owners' different tastes and dispositions, became places for recording the personalities

■ The Summer Palace, Beijing, in winter.

and tastes of the scholars. Not only the garden building techniques and the plants and water scenes in the gardens, but even the halls, buildings, pavilions, boats, kiosks, corridors and bridges all contained their owners' hopes, instant thoughts, hidden ambition or bodhi (Buddhist state of enlightenment). For example, pavilions could be square, rectangular, round, pentagonal, hexagonal, quincuncial, cross-shaped, fan-shaped, a square inside a circle and concentric circles. The gates and doors are rectangular, round, octagonal or of other shapes. As to the windows, there are more than 1,000 types of lattice windows in the gardens of Suzhou, with each having its own characteristics and looking like a painting by borrowing outside scenes.

This is an infinite world. After entering a garden, visitors linger over a palatial hall, corridors, screens, rockery caves, stone walls, waterfall, brooks, plank roads, pavilions, ponds or a painted pleasure boat — all of which look different depending on the changing seasons and the time of the day. Even a swallow's nest under the eave of a hall or the wings of a dragonfly can be fascinating in such surroundings.

Garden of the Creator

The philosophy of the correspondence between man and heaven lay behind the planning of gardens.

Classic Chinese gardens were basically imitations of natural scenes. If possible, most of the landscape would be preserved, and included in a new ecological order. The human contribution would be hidden in one way or another.

Although lakes were excavated, hills built, dams constructed and swamps drained, these traces of human labor would surely be covered up by planting trees and flowers. Sometimes, of course, human labor was used intentionally to imitate natural landscapes or create artistic concepts found in landscape paintings or poems. The essence of a poem was its lack of "distance" from Nature, according to the Qing Dynasty scholar Wang Guowei. This lack of "distance" means that there was no conflict with and no estrangement from Nature. This is even truer of a painting.

Exotic rocks and stones are common sights in classical Chinese gardens. Such rocks and stones contain absolutely no human labor, but were created by Nature itself. Human efforts to improve upon Nature were regarded as futile. When human labor is evident, it is in an auxiliary role, such as giving

■ The Gaze-at-the-Mountains Pavilion in the Canglang Garden, Suzhou.

a name to an exotic rock, carving out a door or a window or writing couplets for pavilion columns.

Borrowing Scenes

Classical Chinese gardens are unique in shape, and rich in architectural technique. But even in an elaborate and gorgeous garden there is nothing superfluous. Just as a

■ The Kunming Lake in Summer Palace, Beijing.

superb piece of writing in which no essential word must be omitted, and no unnecessary word must be included. Of the more than 1,000 lattice windows in the famous gardens of Suzhou, none was put there unintentionally. On the contrary, they provide the viewer with multifarious changes, with scenes inside scenes, boundaries without boundaries, apparently divided but not divided, their sizes contrasted, and both inside and outside mutually apparent.

The garden designers arranged the layout of the garden scenery so that "there are hills and gullies in the mind". Such arrangements made it possible to organize and create space freely. The common technical terms such as borrowing scenes, dividing scenes and separating scenes all indicate applications of specific techniques, and can also be developed on the

■ Hall for Old People of Great Virtue in the Lingering Garden, Suzhou.

spot by taking the best advantage of the situation in the course of practice. For example, "borrowing scenes" refers to designs of borrowing remote scenes, nearby scenes, scenes by looking up, scenes by looking down, and scenes reflected in mirrors.

For example, standing on the east side of the lake in the Summer Palace and looking to the west, we can see a very beautiful tower in the Western Hills, and think that it is in the Summer Palace itself. But in fact, the tower is on the Yuquan (Jade Fountain) Hill. This is a "borrowed scene". Likewise, the lake is so long from north to south that all the Western Hills that can be seen from the palace are reflected in the lake. The peach and willow trees on the causeways were placed on purpose where they would hide the enclosing wall in the west, so that the boundary between the palace and the surrounding countryside would disappear. Moreover, the Western Hills, the trees on the causeways and the shadow of the tower on Yuquan Hill join together naturally as part of the scenery of the garden. The use of doors, rocks and walls to create the winding and in-depth atmosphere and many changes is "dividing the scenes". The Garden of Harmonious Interest in the

Summer Palace is a small garden inside a big garden. This is a "separated scene".

Whether borrowed scenes, contrasting scenes, separated scenes or divided scenes, they were all intended to make use of the arrangement and replacement of space to correspond to the changes in the soul and mind. Chinese garden art is particularly good in this respect. Its unique aesthetics do not permit monotonous repetition or any dullness beyond three steps. It always tries to enable people to see new and different scenes as the viewer moves. In his *Six Chapters of a Floating Life*, Shen Fu says, "See small in the big, and big in the small, real in the false and false in the real, either hidden or exposed, either shallow or deep, and not only circling, winding, bending and folding ." This is typical of the aspiration of Chinese arts in general, and not just the art of garden design.

■ Interior scene of the palace in Norbu Linka (summer palace of the Dalai Lamas), Lhasa, Tibet Autonomous Region.

Wangchuan Garden

Touring mountains and rivers to enjoy the beauty of Nature was a particular delight of old Chinese scholars. Zhang Dai of the Ming Dynasty said, "I'm fond of the study, beautiful maids, handsome boys, new clothes, delicious food, fine horses, colorfully decorated lanterns, fireworks, the Pear Garden, orchestral music, antiques, birds and flowers." These were indeed his lifetime pursuits. After the fall of the Ming Dynasty, he spent his time deep in the mountains, where he could see even more interesting things as the seasons changed.

Most of the famous classical gardens in China were built in the Ming and Qing dynasties, and the best of them are in the Yangtze River Delta. Because of its fine climate, the delta was

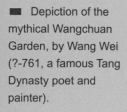
■ Depiction of the mythical Wangchuan Garden, by Wang Wei (?-761, a famous Tang Dynasty poet and painter).

a favorite place to visit for aristocrats and officials of all dynasties during their southern tours. Since aristocrats went there, scholars also swarmed there.

The position of scholars in ancient China was a precarious one. They did not always have a chance to serve their country, and their official positions always depended on luck. Therefore, few of their poems and essays are pure landscape poetry or travel notes, because they always contained something weighing on their minds, some deeply hidden resentment. They were always fond of gardens and miniature landscapes, because they could control their surroundings in this way. In gardens were pines, cypresses, plum trees and other symbols of longevity, which could be allowed to grow by waters, have hanging branches and twigs or drape over cliffs, could be made straight, slanting, bent or supine, could be made to dry up and wither, and could be trimmed and cut. Xu Youren of the Yuan Dynasty said, "Two slender bamboos stand by one rock, and there have always been endless poems in the past and today."

Scholars with no official ranks could not buy land to build their own gardens, so they built gardens in their hearts in different ways to blend themselves with Nature. For example, Zheng Banqiao of the Qing Dynasty was fond of bamboos, and Mi Fu of the Northern Song Dynasty worshipped stones. Wang Wei, a great poet of the Tang Dynasty who became a successful official in his early years, built the famous Wangchuan Garden. It was a natural garden with woods and springs. In his "Writing to Pei Di in the Mountains", he told his friend, "To the north is the Bahe River, with the city walls reflected in the water in the clear moonlight. Climbing to the top of Huazi Ridge at night, I see the Wanghe River rippling in the moonbeams. A distant fire twinkles outside the woods in the cold mountains. Dogs bark in the darkness, with cries as loud as those of leopards. When spring comes, the grass and trees grow luxuriantly, and the mountains are clearly

■ Traditional wooden bed with landscape paintings.

visible. The water flows gently, and the white gulls fly with their wings spread proudly." This landscape master, who was proficient in Buddhist tenets and poetry and good at painting, made his scholarly garden pure, elegant and free from worldly affairs — the characteristics of his natural and unaffected poems. This might have been the highest manifestation of Nature in the minds of the literati of all dynasties, who constantly sang the praises of the moon and wind, drank wine, composed poems and looked for plum blossoms while walking in the snow.

Chapter **10**

Furniture of the East

Looking for Sandalwood

The feelings of the Chinese people for wood are embodied very concretely in their furniture. They all like wood with a special property. For example, traditionally a kind of wood called eagle's tea shrub was used for making cupboards, because such wood can prevent food from being spoiled. Cypress wood was used for making coffins, because it was resistant to decay. Sandalwood was used for making axe

■ Chair carved out of a single piece of wood.

handles, because it is strongly resistant to deformation, thus enhancing safety. Red sandalwood has always been called the "king of wood". It grows extremely slowly. In fact, there is a folk saying that the tree grows one inch in 100 years, and only becomes useful timber after it grows five inches. However, the sandalwood tree tends to become hollow as it matures, and so the older it gets the less use can be made of the timber. This makes sandalwood a rare item, and in the past it could only be used by the imperial court. Examples of sandalwood used in buildings and furniture can be seen in the Forbidden City, the Summer Palace and the Beihai Imperial Garden (now Beihai Park) in Beijing.

Red sandalwood contains a considerable amount of oil, which helps it to resist cracking. Moreover, the natural veins of the wood make it attractive enough to make painting or other furbishing superfluous, and its hard texture and fine fibers make it ideal for carving. As a result, it was already very hard to find the wood in the later years of the Qing Dynasty, and it was often looked for in other countries.

The rareness of red sandalwood and the prohibition against its use by ordinary people sparked a search for substitutes. As many as a dozen species of red woods were

■ Wooden horses dating from the Western Han Dynasty, unearthed at Mianyang, Sichuan Province, showing the reproductive organs of male horses.

used in the old days, such as suanzhi wood, old red wood, new red wood, fragrant red wood, Chinese yew, huali wood (Onmosia henryi), new huali wood and old huali wood.

Grains and Painting

As early as in the Neolithic Age, the Chinese learned the properties of paints and pigments. During the Shang and Zhou dynasties the application of Chinese lacquer had already reached a high standard, being applied in daily-use and handicraft articles and artistic works. Lacquer is a natural sap obtained from several kinds of varnish trees. Its main constituents are phenol, enzyme, resin and water. Varnish is moisture-resistant, and resistant to high temperatures and corrosion. It can be given various colors, and preserves its gloss indefinitely.

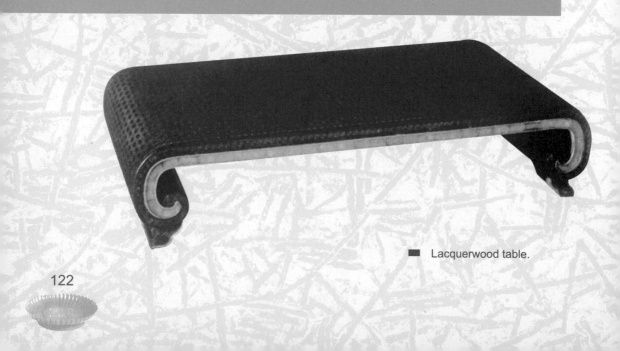

■ Lacquerwood table.

■ Boxwood pen container.

The Chinese people have always liked lively images of animals in their decorations of buildings and furniture, especially dragons, tigers, birds and snakes. Plant designs are also found on furniture, but they became popular only after the founding of the Tang Dynasty.

■ Red-lacquered box in the shape of a chrysanthemum petal.

Mortise and Tenon Joints

A mortise and tenon joint is a method of fixing two sections of wood, bamboo or even stone by inserting the projecting part of one into a hole carved in another. The projecting part is called the tenon and the hole is called the mortise.

Because of the wide territory and multitude of ethnic groups in China, common terms for the object differ greatly in local dialects. Common terms for the mortise and tenon include: zongjiao (brown corner) tenon, baojian (shoulder holding) tenon, jiatou (head clamping) tenon, chajian (shoulder

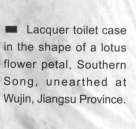

■ Lacquer toilet case in the shape of a lotus flower petal, Southern Song, unearthed at Wujin, Jiangsu Province.

■ Wooden tenons unearthed from the New Stone Age ruins in Hemudu, Yuyao, Zhejiang Province.

inserting) tenon, gejian tenon, baojiao (corner holding) tenon, tou (infiltration) tenon, dovetail tenon, gougua (hook) tenon, yandaiguo (pipe bowl) tenon, and also luoguo (arched) post and bawang (dominant) post.

The tendency of the mortise and tenon joint to follow nature and its practical use in joining wooden members can be regarded as the soul of wooden furniture. Just like the soul of Chinese culture, it is hidden very deep. It originally rejects dismantling, but an outsider can only dismantle it before he can see it clearly. The problem is that no matter how good it is it may become useless after being dismantled. Such also often happens in traditional culture.

Mortise and tenon joints have been found in the *Paleolithic Hemudu Ruins*. Already at that time, both dovetail and straight tenons were used, apparently used on members that bore different weights. This invention allowed the erection of large buildings without using a single nail.

There are six methods of using a mortise and tenon joint to join wooden members: cutting a tenon on the column head or column foot; joining the horizontal members like an architrave with the vertical members like columns; join wooden members with a tenon cut on one end and a mortise cut on another; straight joint at right angles for the horizontal and vertical members; splicing of two overlapping members with holes cut in the same positions for bolting; and using blocks on brackets.

The mortise and tenon technique raised the artistic value of Chinese-style furniture. The absence of nails prolongs the life of the wood.

Furniture of Ming and Qing Dynasties

The Ming and Qing dynasties were a golden age for Chinese traditional furniture. Painting skills and techniques developed to an unparalleled height, stressing natural veins and glossy colors. As a result, the furniture made during this period came to be viewed as an art form.

During this period, huali wood (Onmosia henryi) and red sandalwood were shipped from Southeast Asia to China in large quantities. Moreover, as hardwood furniture became the first choice of the imperial family, the taste for hardwood spread widely. Furniture was embellished with lacquer and enamel, and inlays of gold, jade, ceramics, asparagus plumosus and shells, as well as precious stones and pearls.

Ming furniture was characterized by its wide variety and generous shaping. This can be regarded as the mature period of traditional Chinese furniture. The Palace Museum in Beijing and the classical gardens in Suzhou all have large collections of Ming furniture. Suzhou was the starting and returning point of the seven voyages made by the great Ming navigator Zheng He, who sailed as far as the east coast of Africa. In exchange for Chinese silk and porcelain ware, Zheng He brought back, among other things, large amounts of redwood and other hard woods. Such timber was preferred because it was very heavy and helped stabilize the ships, which became lighter as their trading wares were unloaded.

The Ming Dynasty opened a new era for the furniture, and its typical characteristic was the development of hardwood items. Prior to this, Chinese furniture either stressed painting or complicated shapes and structures, but Ming furniture returned to ancient simplicity and elegance. This was because of the qualities of hardwood. Compared with Western furniture, which stressed carving and the inlaying of the grains, Ming furniture paid attention to the softness and smoothness of the meeting between the human body and the furniture.

■ Chair made of Onmosia henryi wood, Qing Dynasty.

Inheriting this tradition, the Qing Dynasty assimilated foreign styles, and gradually created Guangzhou-style, Suzhou-style and Beijing-style furniture.

In summary, furniture was clumsy and crude in the Shang and Zhou dynasties. The development of low furniture convenient for sitting emerged in the Spring and Autumn and Warring States periods, and the Qin and Han dynasties, and elegance came to the fore during the period of Wei, Jin and the Northern and Southern Dynasties. In the Tang time, the furniture was as beautiful as the national custom. In the Song Dynasty, the furniture was simple and elegant and lofty, perhaps influenced by the Confucian school of idealist philosophy. The Ming Dynasty laid the foundation for the prosperous development of classical Chinese furniture. Variant styles appeared during the elegant and poised Qing Dynasty.

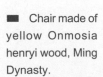
■ Chair made of yellow Onmosia henryi wood, Ming Dynasty.

Chapter 11

Chopsticks
as the Fulcrum

Lengthened Fingers

An honorary professor of the University of California once said, "The three categories of people who use knives and forks, fingers and chopsticks, respectively, all strongly defend their own customs." The method of eating can reveal many details of a nation. In the multitude of nationalities, the Chinese are the most famous chopstick users. A foreigner who admires Chinese culture makes his first contact with the culture when he begins to learn to use chopsticks.

 Wooden container for chopsticks.

Sometimes, the skillfulness of using chopsticks is always synchronized with learning to speak Chinese. When one can speak Chinese well, one is almost always very good at using chopsticks. The main reason for failing to use chopsticks well lies in the fact that it is a natural way of behavior inherent in the culture. This is like learning to sing Peking opera. Perhaps it is not difficult for you to shout out a few words, but a line of a libretto is much more difficult to master, because the words themselves cannot get away from the cultural environment they sprang up in, and need a proper ecological space. This is the breathing or the air flow itself which a nation is accustomed to. The inhaling and exhaling, the power of control, and everything related to the tune will be assembled. It is a matter of using the sound to draw a portrait, and using the real air for wafting a civilization. The recessive mystery of the exchange is interlinked with the smoothness and vigor of calligraphy or the perfect coordination of the energy and the pulse. It may also communicate with the artistic conception of poetry or the manual skills of carpenters. In fact, it is very easy for people to associate this with table tennis, which stresses perfect cooperation between the mind and the hands. It can be compared with Chinese chess or weiqi (go), exquisite handicraft products, acrobatics, gymnastics or diving, none of which requires sheer physical strength. They need similar balanced and symmetrical manual skills to those needed when using chopsticks.

Chopsticks vs. Knife and Fork

For the origin of chopsticks, Cai Yuanpei, once president of Peking University, said, "As early as more than 3,000 years ago, the ancestors of the Chinese people also used knives and forks. But later, knives and forks came to be regarded as lethal weapons. Moreover, Chinese cookery had been greatly improved, and there was no longer any need to cut meat into small pieces at mealtimes. Therefore, beginning in the Shang Dynasty, knives and forks were replaced by chopsticks."

Westerners use knives and forks as dining utensils, with the knife held in the right hand and the fork in the left. They look gentle and refined. Using glasses and plates, they cut everything in front of them piece by piece with the knife and fork them into the mouth while talking and chatting.

The Chinese use bamboo chopsticks as their dining utensils. A group of people, sitting around a table, use three fingers to hold the chopsticks with a flexible and mild motion, and obediently lift food from bowls without difficulty. They don't have to worry about cutting their fingers.

Bamboo chopsticks are in motion. They survive in the universe in a poetic way and with human interest, and they survive with Chinese philosophical appeal. The hands moving the chopsticks form a philosophical picture of Heaven, Earth and Man in motion. This picture will never be completed. As long as the universe is not extinct, it will keep on creating, just like the Buddhist doctrine of creation — with the mind as

■ Wooden food boxes
and chopsticks.

a mirror, the mountains, rivers, the sun, the moon and the stars move freely. Besides, the birds, beasts, insects, fish, flowers, grasses, trees, winds, clouds, thunderbolts and lightning appear now and then.

The Chinese arts emerged exactly from this. The soul is born and grows with Nature, bright and colorful, all the year round, and returns to Nature. Art is expanded by Nature, Nature injected with soul and vigor. Art survives by relying on Nature, just as chopsticks do, as they were born in a bamboo forest.

Taboos and Superstition

The Chinese and the Italians both eat noodles. When Italians eat spaghetti, they use a fork to lift the noodles and turn them with the wrist several times. Then they place the noodles carefully in the mouth. They must be very careful in this whole process. But they cannot eat spaghetti in hot soup, because it's not easy to turn the fork, and it's possible to knock over the bowl. But the Chinese do not have such trouble when eating noodles.

I wonder if the Westerners worship the knife and fork, or even take them as totems. The Chinese certainly have a lot of taboos and superstitions concerning chopsticks. For example, you must not lay the chopsticks across the bowl after finishing your meal, because this would indicate that you are not yet full. From the position of the fingers on the chopsticks one can judge a man's marriage date. When a new-born baby is 100 days old, the elders use a chopstick to make a red dot between his or her eyebrows as a symbol of good luck.

When the construction of a new house reaches the stage of placing the main beams, the carpenter traditionally uses a red thread to tie seven chopsticks together. He then hangs them on the main beam over the front door.

After 49 days, all devils in the area of the construction are regarded as having been dispelled, and the new house is then considered to be safe and lucky.

Chinese culture has never been short of gods and devils, and many of them are related to eating. Why? I think it is because food is always an important matter to a nation laden with calamities. Sayings go: "People regard food as their prime want," "Thunderbolts never hit diners," "The well-fed don't know how the starving suffer," and even before a man was to be beheaded, he was offered wine and meat, so that he would not become a hungry devil in the afterlife. In the countryside, children used to be taught that they would never get married if they ate pig's feet, and would have lice if they ate sesame seeds. Such warnings were presumably to guard against children eating too much as a waste of such food.

There were also taboos for adults. The classic novel *The Scholars* describes how a country magistrate invites Fan Jin to dinner, but the latter refuses to use the silver chopsticks provided for him, considering them too exalted for him to use in front of a man of the magistrate rank. When the silver chopsticks are replaced with a pair of ivory ones, Fan Jin still refuses to use them, and only when plain wooden chopsticks are brought does he start to eat.

Chapter **12**

The Final Lodging

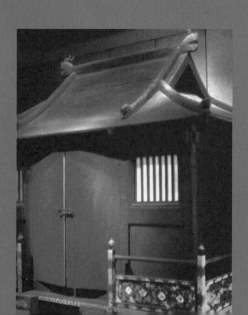

Mystery of Cliff Coffins

In the Wuyi Mountains of Fujian Province and in parts of Jiangxi, Zhejiang, Taiwan, Hunan, Hubei, Sichuan, Guizhou, Yunnan, Guangdong and Hainan provinces, as well as the Guangxi Zhuang Autonomous Region, there used to be a custom of suspending the coffins containing the remains of the deceased high upon cliff sides, or in rock crevices or

■ Suspended coffins in Matangba, Gongxian County, Sichuan Province.

138

man-made caves. According to textual research, the history of suspended coffins covers all the periods from the Shang Dynasty to the Qing Dynasty, and this custom was mainly practiced by the ethnic-minority people in the south of China. The phenomenon was first noticed by Gu Yewang of the Northern and Southern Dynasties when he visited the Wuyi Mountains, and wrote about "several thousand suspended coffins on the cliffs".

A legend about the suspended coffins prevalent among the people of the She ethic group living in Fujian Province goes like this: In the remote past King Pan Hu, ancestor of the She people, married the third daughter of Emperor Gao Xin, and had three sons and a daughter by her. The family moved to Fenghuang (Phoenix) Mountain to do hunting and farming. Because King Pan Hu was born of a constellation, he could not go into the earth when he died. Therefore, after his death his children and grandchildren used carriage wheels and ropes to hoist his coffin into a cliff cave on the mountain.

A legend of the Bo people in southwest China says that when plague threatened they would be protected from it by burying their dead in the rocks, which they worshipped. The protection extended to the coffins by the cliffs was supposed to bring good luck to the offspring of the deceased.

In his book *China's Suspended Coffin Burials*, Chen Mingfang enumerated many other related stories. According to the *Records of Anecdotes and Interesting Episodes at Court and Among the Populace* by Zhang Zhuo of the Tang Dynasty, "To lay the dead to rest in high places is to show filial piety."

It is interesting to note that most of the suspended coffins are hung on riverside cliffs, and the coffins themselves tend to be shaped like dugout canoes, indicating that the people who practiced this custom had an affinity with rivers.

Outlook on Death in the East

■ Wooden coffin cover made in the 10th century, now kept in the Museum of Liaoning Province.

Another mysterious phenomenon connected with death in ancient China is the "sun-shaped" group of graves discovered at the location of the Kingdom of Kroraina near the Kongque (Peacock) River in Xinjiang, dating back some 3,800 years. Poplar wood stakes were used to form seven concentric circles around the graves some two meters deep, the whole looking like a radiant sun. The feet of the occupants of the graves all face west.

Voltaire said, in his debate with Jean J. Rousseau, that China had built the Great Wall 200 years before Christ, but failed to prevent the Tartars from breaching it. China's Great Wall has often been regarded as a monument of fear. The Pyramids of Egypt are monuments of emptiness and superstition. What both show is the great patience of those nations, not their wisdom.

The ancient Chinese patriarchal clan system dictated that not only should the living congregate in kinship groups, but that the dead must also be buried together. And even the location and arrangement of the graves depended on the rank of the deceased in the family and clan hierarchies. This can even be traced in the layouts and locations of the imperial temples and palaces.

Confucius said, "If you don't know how to live, how can you know how to die?" Thus, from the beginning, the question of death was almost completely excluded from the deliberations of the philosophers in China.

An extreme example of a Chinese philosopher's indifference to death is found in *Zhuangzi*. When Zhuangzi's disciples came to express condolences over the death of his wife, they found Zhuangzi drumming on an upturned earthen basin and singing cheerfully.

 Later, as Zhuangzi was dying, he admonished his disciples as they were discussing the arrangements for his funeral. "After I die," he said, "use Heaven and Earth for my coffin, the sun and the moon as my jade burial objects, and the stars as my pearls. Since I will then have everything to accompany me, what else should I desire?" His disciples said, "We are afraid that the hawks will eat your flesh."

Zhuangzi replied with a smile, as he bid farewell to them, "I would be eaten by hawks if I were left on the ground. But under the ground there are ants. Why should I be taken out of the mouths of the hawks only to be delivered over to the ants?"

The story goes that, when the famous poet Su Shi read about the drunkard Liu Ling, who insisted that his servant carried a hoe with him so that he could be buried on the spot where he fell down dead after becoming drunk, Su Shi said with a laugh, "Why should a man be buried after death? This shows how hypocritical the famous scholars in the Wei and Jin dynasties were!"

It is said that Lu Ban the master carpenter once devised machinery which allowed the sealing up of the corpse. It is also said that he could tell when a man would die from the type of coffin he was asked to make for him. This peculiar skill is still claimed by some coffin makers today, and many people make preparations for their death according to the carpenter's forecast.

The ultimate ambition among traditionally minded Chinese villagers was to have a fine coffin made of spruce wood. If a man's relatives did not think the coffin sufficiently grand, they might delay the burial until a more suitable one was purchased.

In some southern parts of China, people even give a coffin as a gift, because the Chinese pronunciation of coffin is "guancai", homonymous for "achieving official position and making a fortune". This is another example of the complexities of Chinese culture.

Chapter **13**

Wood Artistry

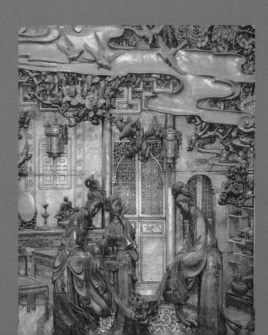

Wood Carving

The most famous types of Chinese wood carving are the Dongyang-style wood carving of Zhejiang Province, the gold lacquer wood carving of Guangdong Province, the boxwood carving of Wenzhou, Zhejiang Province, and the Longyan wood carving of Fujian Province. Other well-known styles include the kan wood carving of Qufu, the imitation of ancient wood carving of Nanjing, the redwood carving of Suzhou, the Jianchuan wood carving of Yunnan, the white wood carving of Shanghai, the birch wood carving of Yongling and the colored wood carving of Quanzhou.

These different traditions are distinguished by their distinct local characteristics,

■ Dongyang wood carving from Zhejiang Province, named "Story of the White Lady".

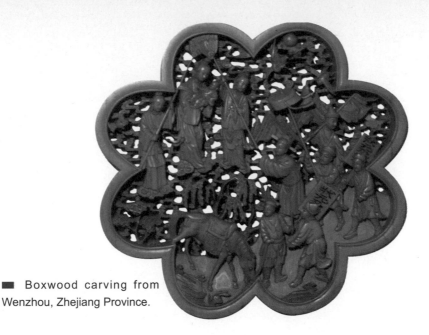

■ Boxwood carving from Wenzhou, Zhejiang Province.

choice of raw material and craftsmanship. For example, the boxwood carving of Wenzhou, influenced by the style and lines of the paintings of the literati in the declining years of the Qing Dynasty, is known for its unsophisticated and smooth cutting techniques, composition of the false and the real, and poetic appeal.

Wood carving is generally divided into art carving and practical carving. The latter include lanterns and lamps, screens, mirror stands, penholders, picture frames, clock stands, jewelry boxes and niches for Buddhist statues, as well as architectural parts, furniture and other handicraft articles. Generally, they are designed and carved by experienced artists and carvers, and reproduced by skilled workers in large quantities. Therefore, there are certain standards and formulae for the subject matters and forms of expression. The work processes are also very clear and explicit: making blanks, trimming, polishing, glossing and preparing a proper base for the carving. Of course, the most crucial part is the designing, at the very beginning.

The Story of Wood

Artistic wood carving is marked by more design elements. Because it is art, the originality, aesthetic concept, artistic method, artistic skill of the carver, and his inspiration and superb skills are fundamental to the success or failure of this type of wood carving. Like other plastic arts, it follows the paths of realism, simulation, exaggeration, abstraction or deformation, proceeding from the form and attributes of the primary material — wood. On the basis of the natural pattern and natural veins of the wood, a pictographic image is conceived, and the workman uses his skills according to the nature of the material, either cutting with bold and powerful strokes or working with meticulous care and precision or applying skills in a natural way with brevity.

Certain materials show extraordinary external forms at first sight, and some require painstaking thinking. This is why we say, "Seventy percent is the natural form and 30 percent is the carving." The simplest way of attaining an idea for an artistic carving is to choose wood of grotesque forms and shapes. Then look at them closely, until an original idea forms in the mind. A good wood carving gives a sudden sense of beauty, just like a superb poem. Even if it is very simple, its pure image and instant feeling can give people endless aesthetic pleasure. In short, a good wood carving, just like any other work of art, is a work of superb craftsmanship excelling Nature, an expression of individuality. However, its difference from other arts is that a good piece of wood carving always looks as if it were not yet completely finished. Its artistic quality shows the tendency of the artistic efforts leaning to the diffusion of the natural essence because of the seemingly unfinished effect.

Wood carvings can be divided into "independent" and

"attached" works. The "independent" carvings are individual and independent works of art. Usually, they are interior furnishings or table ornaments. "Attached" carvings are mainly accessories to other objects or works of art made for the spaces of interior walls or doors and windows. The slight projection of the cut part is called low relief, and the deeply cut projection from the base is called high relief. Relief carving with the wood around the relief pierced through so that it produces an effect of a papercut is called openwork. The gradation of the composition of the carving is complicated. Carving with the fore part being detached in space and theme from the background is called "toutong" carving in China。 Examples can be found in the wood carving of the Bai ethnic group of Jianchuan, Yunnan Province, in the Jinmabiji Mill in Kunming, the Feilai Temple in Baoshan, the Bajiao Pavilion in Erhai and the Jizushan Temple.

Legend of the Pear Garden

According to the records in the *New Tang Annals*, Emperor Ming of the Tang Dynasty trained 300 musicians and several hundred maids to perform in the Pear Garden. The expression "Pear Garden"

■ Puppet "The Emperor's Younger Sister".

The Story of Wood

then became a synonym for theatrical troupes and theaters, and the emperor was honored as the founder of theatrical troupes.

Wooden masks are an integral part of many of China's stage genres, including Tibetan, Jiangzhou, Kunqu and Nuo operas.

Traditional puppets are also made of wood. It is said that puppet shows first appeared in the Han Dynasty, and have been popular ever since, especially in the countryside. The puppets are easy to transport, and the shows can be given in flexible forms. Classical puppet performances include *Lotus Flower Fairy, Scholar Zhang Meets the Dragon King's Daughter at Sea, The Monkey King Beats the White Bone Demon Three Times, Ne Zha Disturbs the Sea, The Monkey King Borrows the Palm-Leaf Fan Three Times, Big Lin and Little Lin, Wild Swan, Small Bell, Storming Heaven, A Rat Marries*

■ Picture of a traditional big-drum performance, consisting of singing to the accompaniment of a drum, Qing Dynasty.

Off His Daughter, The Eight Immortals Cross the Sea, Wang Xiao'er Kills a Tiger, Pigsy Carries His Sweetheart on His Back, Crane and Tortoise and *The Little Cowherd.*

Burning incense is a central part of Chinese folk customs. Incense was burned to show reverence for the ancestors, the gods, the Buddha, the immortals, animals, mountains, rivers, trees and stones. The rite of burning incense was developed in China roughly in three stages: Before the reign of Emperor Wu of the Han Dynasty, incense was only used during sacrifices to the gods or ancestors. From then until the Three Kingdoms period, incense was burned on any solemn occasion. And later, incense was burned not only on formal occasions but also as a way to freshen the air in a house.

Traditional Musical Instruments

There are few ethnic groups in China having fewer than 10 traditional musical instruments each. Most of traditional Chinese musical instruments are made of wood, including erhu (two-shinged fiddle), guzheng (pluck instrument with 21

■ Seven-stringed wooden zither.

The Story of Wood

■ Four-stringed
lutes of the Yi people.

■ Pipa.

or 25 strings), pipa (pluck instrument with a fretted finger board), dongxiao (vertical bamboo flute), guqin (seven-stringed pluck instrument), ruan (pluck stringed instrument) and sanxuan (three-stringed pluck instrument).

It seems that the ancient Chinese thought that wood itself could sing. This explains the "wooden fish", a piece of wood tapped by monks and folk ballad singers to give out a distinct sound.

The traditional music of the Yi people involves beating on a log of wood in time with their footsteps.

The Pumi people of Yunnan Province cherish a four-stringed pluck instrument. Legend has it that long ago a young man named Abu was in love with a beautiful girl named Anai, but the girl cared nothing for him. The sad

■ Wooden wind musical instruments, Ming Dynasty.

young man carved a piece of wood into the shape of a human head, attached strings to it, and played a mournful tune. Four days later, Anai, much moved, consented to become Abu's wife.

■ Guzheng, a pluck musical instrument with 21 or 25 strings.

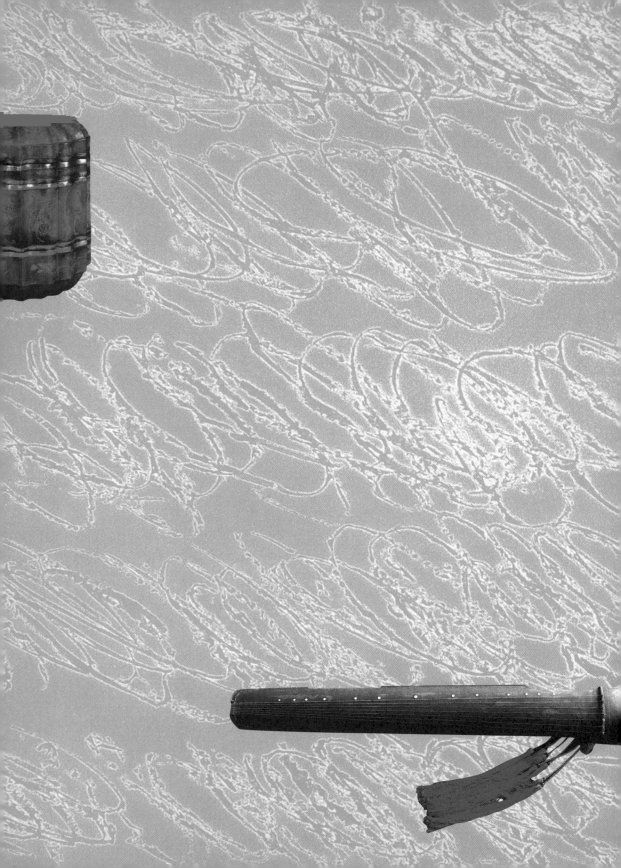

Chapter **14**

Vessels on the Sea

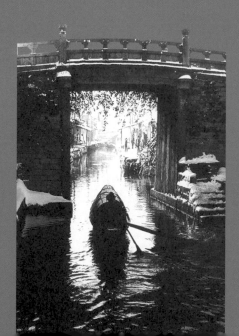

Sail on a Raft

In the book *Shi Ben*, Liu Xiang claims that the ancient Chinese got the idea of building boats from observing how leaves float on water. This led them to devise rafts, with which to traverse rivers and even to cross stretches of ocean. Confucius said, "If my teachings are not accepted, I'll embark on a raft, and sail overseas."

During the Spring and Autumn and Warring States periods, boats were of great strategic value to the rival rulers, and the boat building industry and navigation developed rapidly. According to the *Annals of Yue*, when the State of Yue moved its capital from Kuaiji to Langya, it built rafts of pine and cypress, manned them with 2,800 sailors, and transported the court northward along the coast. During the Qin Dynasty, Xu Fu and 3,000 virgin boys and 3,000 virgin girls took to sea in ships to seek the pills of immortality. The first international maritime trade route in the world commenced operation during the Western Han Dynasty. Known as the "Maritime Silk Road", it began at the ancient prefecture of Hepu in southeast China, and stretched as far as India and Sri Lanka. During the period of the Three Kingdoms, Sun Quan sent generals Wei

Wen and Zhuge Zhi with 10,000 troops in ships to explore Taiwan and Japan.

Wooden boats were first propelled with paddles, then with oars and rudders, and finally with sails.

During the latter period of the Eastern Jin Dynasty, the Buddhist monk Faxian traveled westward to India in search of Buddhist scriptures. After an absence of 14 years, he returned home by sea at the age of 70. When the scriptures were translated into Chinese, they had a profound effect on the development of Buddhism in China.

■ Typical river scene in Shaoxing.

Emperor Yang of the Sui Dynasty (581-618) engaged in an ambitious boat-building program. The biggest of these vessels, consisting of four decks, was 15 meters high and nearly 70 meters long. On the top deck were the main hall, the emperor's quarters and rooms for affairs of state. On the third and second decks were 120 rooms "painted with red plaster, decorated in gold and green with ornaments made of pearls and jade, and carved and engraved beautifully".

During the Tang Dynasty, shipbuilding technology made great strides, with the adoption of the mortise-and-tenon joint, watertight cabins, caulking and ballasting. Iron anchors were widely used. The warships at that time were called louchuan, mengchong, doujian, zouke, haijuan and youting, and the biggest warship built at that time, known as a hezhouzai, took three years to complete. It could carry 3,000 soldiers.

The "Maritime Silk Road" enjoyed a new period of prosperity during the Tang Dynasty, and the Tang capital, Chang'an, became an international metropolis. Envoys,

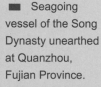
■ Seagoing vessel of the Song Dynasty unearthed at Quanzhou, Fujian Province.

students, monks and merchants from other countries came to learn from China's advanced culture, political systems and institutions. Overseas, the Chinese people were called "Tang people". As the most powerful developed country in the world at that time, China opened shipping routes to Southeast Asia, West Asia and Eastern Africa. It was during the Tang Dynasty too that Chinese monks went to Japan to spread Buddhism.

During the following Song and Yuan dynasties, as a result of expanding overseas trade, maritime and inland river transport far exceeded that in the previous dynasties, and the shipbuilding industry developed by leaps and bounds. Zhejiang, Fujian and Guangdong provinces became ship-building centers, and the cities of Mingzhou, Guangzhou, Quanzhou and Hangzhou thrived on this industry. In the Song Dynasty sliding rails were used for the first time for launching ships.

Marco Polo, a traveler from Venice, stayed in China for 17 years and gained the favor of the Yuan Dynasty emperor Kublai Khan. In 1291 the khan sent him to escort an imperial bride to Persia by the sea. His fleet, composed of 13 ships with four masts and 12 sails each, sailed from Quanzhou.

Zheng He's Voyages to the West

Zheng He was born into a Muslim family in Kunming, Yunnan Province, in 1371. As a high-ranking eunuch at the court of Emperor Chengzu of the Ming Dynasty, he was sent by the emperor on seven exps in command of huge fleets to foster trade and diplomatic relations with countries to the south and west of China.

In the 28 years from 1405 to 1433, Zheng He visited more than 30 countries in Southeast and South Asia, Iran and Arabia, and even reached the east coast of Africa. Wherever he went, he presented valuable gifts from the Ming emperor to the rulers of those countries, including porcelain ware, silk and silk fabrics, tea, gold, silver, iron ware and farm tools. In return, Zheng He brought back ivory, spices and jewels.

In addition to his trading and diplomatic efforts, Zheng He made great contributions to navigation and geography by drawing up charts of his voyages.

Zheng He's fleets had more than 200 ships each, and carried some 20,000 people. They departed from Taicang in Jiangsu, where most of Zheng He's sailors originated.

About the same time, Fei Xin, also a native of Taicang, visited some 40 countries as an envoy on four missions. After he returned home, he wrote a book called *Seeing Scenic*

■ Reconstruction of one of Zheng He's treasure ships.

Spots from a Raft, which contains his observations of those places.

Why was Zheng He sent on these exps to the West seas? One theory is that Emperor Chengzu, who had usurped the throne, was searching for the whereabouts of his predecessor Emperor Jianwen, who had mysteriously disappeared. Another theory has it that Emperor Chengzu wanted to obtain a relic said to be a tooth of the Buddha, in order to shore up his claim to rule. In fact, Zheng He managed to purchase the relic at an enormous price from the king of Ceylon (modern Sri Lanka).

Be that as it may, Zheng He's seven exps to the southern and western oceans were a landmark in the history of China's exchanges with other countries. China under the Ming Dynasty was already known far and wide as a prosperous and powerful country, and wherever Zheng He went he was received with honors and homage. Hitherto, contacts between China and the West had been conducted mainly by land, through the Silk Road. But Zheng He's exps opened up avenues of contact by sea.

■ Model of an ancient Chinese chariot, with the upright figure serving as a compass.

Maritime Exclusion

However, this glorious period of overseas voyages soon came to a halt. In response to smuggling by foreign merchants and the depredations of Japanese pirates, the Ming government adopted a policy of exclusion. Shipbuilding was tightly controlled, and the few seagoing ships that were allowed to operate were in official hands. This not only stopped Chinese traders collaborating with their foreign counterparts, but also had a severe effect on the maritime fishing industry. As part of this isolationist policy, the Great Wall was strengthened.

An imperial order was issued to the effect that sales of ships with two masts or three masts on the sea would be severely punished on a charge of collaborating with foreign enemies. This lasted until the early years of the Qing Dynasty, leaving the country behind closed doors for several hundred years.

The "four great inventions" of China were used by foreigners to threaten the country which had given rise to them. Warships and guns were sent to China. The cold gleam of the merciless steel soon alarmed this country, still living in the age of "wood".

From the time of Zheng He's exps, which marked the shift of contacts between nations to the sea, all conflicts and wars, and even the modern consciousness itself, were born from the sea. This era caught the Chinese unawares; perhaps they had lived on the land too long.

Chapter **15**

Eternal Fields

Living in the Fields

China is a country which has long attached great importance to moral and poetic traditions, as if all grass and trees, and all mountains and rivers have grown morally. They were all given worldly wisdom. They always interacted with the hearts and souls of human beings. This was the mean, this was serving the state, this was changing one's interest, and this was ingenuity. This was also self-ridicule and self-encouragement. This was the concept that the whole nation

■ Houses built on stilts by the Dai people in Xishuangbanna, Yunnan Province.

was the emperor's family property, the aesthetic gene that every Chinese living in traditional China would inherit, and the identification mark of the traditional Chinese for whom there was no time to emancipate their individuality or personal dignity.

In fact, even today China is still a rural country. This does not refer just to the economy. The economy is, after all, not so complicated a thing, but the philosophy, artistic concept or life aesthetics of the Chinese with their laws and institutions, and their utensils, interest, taste and traditional cognition have given them unbroken ties with the land — just like the roadside grass, the flowers in front of the house and the trees behind the house, or the homes built with wood.

■ Potted wistaria.

Over a very long historical period, Chinese revolutions were more or less agrarian ones. The rebels all came from the land. Therefore, generation after generation, they could only manage to return their hearts to the rural areas and sow them again in the soil. However, they could often only involuntarily lead a wandering life, and only had the memories of their native villages in the remotest corners of their minds, sometimes a piece of peculiar furniture, sometimes

The Story of Wood

a potted landscape or a private garden would take them subconsciously home. Moreover, very often there were some things that had been brought from their native places and kept in conspicuous places. These things needed new sunshine, water and nutriments from the soil of the soul.

Lin Yutang said, "The rural ideal manifested in the arts, philosophy and life, so deeply rooted in the consciousness of the Chinese people, should be a major element for the health of this nation today. Yes, the quintessence of Chinese country life was to strike a balance between the primitive life habits and the civilization. It is the flexibility and moistness of the spirit of the civilization. It transcends reality, but is based on reality."

■ Rural scenery.

People living in the country are not corrupt; only the people living in the cities are corrupt. The scholars and the well-off families who were tired of city life naturally kept singing the praises of the idyllic life. Even today, this has not changed much. Beginning with Yan Zhitui (531-591), and followed by Fan Zhongyan (989-1052), Zhu Xi (1130-1200), Chen Hongmou (1696-1771) and Zeng Guofan (1811-1872), all the leading scholars had famous parental instructions. Their central message was that the noblest family ideals were hard working, purity, and upholding simplicity.

Return to Han and Tang Dynasties

The British literary figure George Bernard Shaw said that of the culture of mankind, half had been destroyed by the partly educated and fully educated people, and the other half by the uneducated. This is another law of the history, which is particularly worth our remembering.

In China, there are many examples of this: Hangzhou is no longer famous for its lake and mountains; the ancient city of Jingzhou is changed

■　A mural in the tomb of Prince Li Chongrun of the Tang Dynasty.

beyond recognition; Shaoxing, a city famous for its waters, bridges, rice wine and Orchid Pavilion, is no longer ancient; Zunyi has put on a new look; Anyang is pierced by a major highway; Xuzhou has demolished its old residential quarters; the famous three mills and seven lanes of Fuzhou have been completely destroyed; the old city of Xi'an is overshadowed by highrise buildings; the 1,000-year-old city wall of Xiangfan was destroyed overnight; the old railway station which was once a symbol of Jinan has been leveled to the ground; and Ningbo has long disappeared, covering under an economic and technical development zone.

A collective memory has been wiped out. We have betrayed our own history. We have gone farther and farther from the wood which we relied and depended on for thousands of

■ Main hall of the Nanchan Temple on Mount Wutai, Shanxi Province, first built in the Tang Dynasty.

years. When tracing the history of the Chinese people, we cannot but recall the prosperous times of the Han and Tang dynasties.

Returning to the history of the Han and Tang dynasties, we are almost at once frightened by a tremendous momentum. We are not simply looking for a kind of self-confidence, which should be the national spirit and strength capable of going to the "ninth heaven above and clasping the five oceans below". Xi'an (Chang'an), Yangzhou, Jingzhou (Yizhou), Anyang or Luoyang, the Yellow Crane Tower or the Tengwang Tower, just by mentioning any city or place at random, I can conjure up in my mind its architectural wonders surpassing the ancient world and amazing the contemporary world. Their undying wood and beautiful images have long stayed in our minds. We have no doubt that if these ancient cities had maintained one-10th of their appearance in the past, they would still amaze the world. In those days there were peace and harmony, and the people lived and worked in contentment. The architecture naturally became the best carrier for the affluence and perfect harmony conveyed or born by the people. There was only the self in the world, and the earth accompanied it. Architecture was the best carrier for the expression of the inner world, wide and bright. The eaves and corbel brackets were the form and spirit. The bricks and tiles, carved with dragons and insects, were the inner strength. The great architecture, the great carpenters' work, the great mettle, the great realm, the great Nature....

The wheel of history cannot be turned back. What can go back, however, is the spirit. In the Han Dynasty, mythology and history were woven into a real world of beautiful things, and sent forth a thrilling momentum and an ancient simplicity.

The Story of Wood

Tang Yongtong has said that the philosophy of the Han Dynasty was cosmology, and the Neo-Confucianism of the Wei and Jin dynasties was ontology. Beginning in the Han Dynasty, represen-tative thinkers and works of philosophy, such as the clas-sic of augury *Huainanzi*, and philosophers like Liu Xin, Yang Xiong, Wang Chong and Wang Fu, all persevered in exploring the origin of the universe, and tried to use qi (vital energy) to link up all things. Qian Mu characterized the experiences in this sphere from the Han Dynasty down to his own times by saying, "The academic thinking in the 300 years of the Wei, Jin and Northern and Southern Dynasties can be summed up as 'The awakening of the individual self'." A story in the *New Collection of Anecdotes of Famous Personages* goes, "Wang Ziyou lived on the northern side of a mountain. A heavy snow fell in the night. He woke up, opened the door, and ordered wine. When he looked around, it was all white. So he ransacked his memory and recited Zuo Si's poem "Inviting Hermits" . He suddenly thought of Dai Andao, but Dai was in Yan at that time. So he took a small boat, and went to see him. He arrived at Dai's house in the morning, but returned without knocking at the door. When he was asked why, Wang replied, 'I went there in high spirits, and did not come back until I enjoyed myself completely. Why did I have to see Dai?'"

The Wei and Jin Dynasties fostered the temperament of "being self-willed and unrestrained," "having a free and indulgent disposition" and "being unbridled in doing anything." In the trend of thought of the times, the individual should simply live naturally. They were artistic subjects, and they were also aesthetic subjects. This is, in fact, another clue to the traditional Chinese personality. Zhuangzi defied and rejected the existentialism and values of Confucian ethics, tried to develop a brand-new state of mind through his own aesthetic interest, potential capacity and free creation, and by returning to Nature tried to "be on an equal level with all things", mix the secular people with Nature to be intimate with each other for the pure aesthetics of the "carefree life". During the Wei and Jin dynasties, the influence of Neo-Confucianism caused Chinese thought to develop gradually toward the aesthetics of the Chan sect of Buddhism. And in its turn, Chan Buddhism emerged as a peculiar key to the opening of the essence of the Tang Dynasty: The personality continued to be developed, and the most famous "artistic mood" in later generations was created in aesthetics. Where did this artistic mood come from? It was often Nature itself, or the "wonderful existence with Nature", or the "contemplation of Nature", and the purpose was to "observe the natural phenomena to perceive the truth", "study the physical world in order to be identical with it", and "to have Nature as the great teacher for life to blend the mind with nature". However, with the advent of the Song Dynasty, the Neo-Confucian school of idealist philosophy blocked many of these roads.

The Laws of Nature

"I guide the mind, the mind guides the eyes, and the eyes guide Mount Hua." This was what one painter learned from his experiences. It was like this that Nature reached the position of the thing-in-itself, step by step. Of course, it was already the thing-in-itself in the earliest times. Laozi said, "Man follows Earth, Earth follows Heaven, Heaven follows the laws, and the laws follow Nature." This naturally refers to a law, an absolute idea. Man is born in Nature. Therefore, he has an inborn sensitivity to Nature. This is also the reason for the juxtaposition of Heaven, Earth and Man.

Zhuangzi continued Laozi's thinking. To enable the people to better develop their natural instincts, Zhuangzi

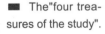
■ The"four treasures of the study".

172

argued that "there are countless things and creatures,
and man can reach the
Great Real only by blending
with Nature". In his remarks
on the art of painting, Zhang
Yanyuan, said, "Meditate
with fixed attention to attain
the realization of Nature.
Forget both outer things and the self,
casting away your body and mind."

Returning to the topic of architecture, the
ultimate and most important principle for Chinese architecture is always to maintain its harmony with Nature,
regardless of your original idea, technological change or
sudden inspiration, they all point to this objective.

■ Cupboard
for tea sets.

The architectural development of the Chinese has resulted in the creation of another Nature. The concept of this
nature is part of the life and art described above — its final
direction is the thing-in-itself of the universe. Therefore, colored drawings, oil paintings, A-shaped roofs, ponds, pairs of
mandarin ducks, the "four treasures of the study", or a grasshopper and cricket painted in golden-yellow and green are all
symbols of joy and happiness in the world. They are part of
the visible world and also part of the other world.

Adhering to this artistic philosophy, which is full of life, we
can also discover that the walls of Chinese temples blend
harmoniously with the green mountains and purple air. The
glazed tiles on the roofs, either light green, dark blue, purple
or golden-yellow, mingle well with the red leaves and clear
sky of the late autumn. They all give us an overall scene of

harmony. This whole scene is the thing-in-itself. Moreover, it will change with the change of the mood of the people who live in it. The rows of trees, the lofty rocks, the depth of water, or the happiness, anger, grief and joy of each flower in the daytime or at night are all blended with the heart to be a part of the Heaven-Earth-Man integrated philosophy.

This spirit can also extend outwardly. For example, the tea drinking habit of the Chinese is surely not limited to dispelling heat or quenching the thirst. It is an integral part of life — an art, in fact. The form of the character "茶" (tea) indicates that man is between grass and a tree. Although tea originally only functioned as a sacrificial oblation, it was used later for cooking and medicine. It was not until the Tang Dynasty that tea was sublimated into the realm of the natural and philosophical. After Lu Yu (733-804) wrote the *Classic of Tea*, more and more particular requirements arose surrounding the drinking of tea: It was desirable to have a "gentle breeze and a bright moon, paper bed-curtain and paper quilt, bamboo bed and stone pillow, exotic flowers and jade trees"

■ Banquet scene.

as true friends, and "literati, monks, Taoist priests, hermits and idle men" as tea drinking companions. When drinking tea, no "bad water, worn-out seats, rough boys or bad maids" should be seen; the best tea should be pleasantly strong and sweet; and when the chemical action stimulates the salivary gland one or two minutes after drinking, an aftertaste should appear. Tea can both help the digestion and calm the emotions. Therefore, it can be said to be a philosophy full of life, a philosophy that can prolong the life of the Chinese people.

The quietness and peace found when drinking tea is a concrete embodiment of the concept of Nature of the Chinese people which can be seen everywhere. At the sight of tea, they will think of the color green, their native places, with the eaves of traditional houses and the spiraling smoke from the kitchens, and recall warm, lasting and significant memories. This is precisely the natural life, the highest pursuit of the Chinese.

Appendix: Reference Books

A Stereotyped Movement, He Ping, Hubei Arts Publishing House, 2002.

Forest of Architecture, Wang Xingguo, China Children's Publishing House, 2001.

China's Ancient Shipbuilding and Navigation, Zhang Jingfen, The Commercial Press, 1997.

Hotels, Pang Pei, Publishing House of the China Federation of Literary and Art Circles, 2002.

The Shadow of Quiet Dreams of the Vernacular, Chang Chao, Shanxi People's Publishing House, 1994.

Housing Culture, Wang Zhenfu and Yang Mingzhi, Fudan University Press, 2001.

Rigid Music, Liang Sicheng, Baihua Literature and Art Publishing House,1998.

History of Ancient Chinese Architecture, Liu Dunzhen, China Building Industry Publishing House, 1980.

Chinese Architectural Aesthetics, Hou Youbin, Heilongjiang Science and Technology Publishing House, 1997.

Ancient Chinese Architecture, Luo Zhewen, Shanghai Classics Publishing House, 1990.

Suzhou's Classical Gardens, Liu Dunzhen, Chinese Building Industry Publishing House, 1979.

Collected Works of Su Manshu, Huacheng Publishing House, 1992.

Dictionary of Chinese and Foreign Classical Arts, Xue Yuan Press, 1989.

Borrowing Wisdom From the Ancients, Gong Pengcheng, Baihua Literature and Art Publishing House, 2005.

My Country and My People, Lin Yutang, Shaanxi Teachers' University Press, 2003.

The Art of Life, Lin Yutang, Shaanxi Teachers' University Press, 2003.

The Life of the Chinese, Lin Yutang, Shaanxi Teachers' University Press, 2003.

Civil Housing, Zhu Ying, Chinese Society Publishing House, 2005.

The Course of Beauty, Li Zehou, China Social Sciences Publishing House, 1986.

Dong Qiao's Prose Works, Zhejiang Literature and Art Publishing House, 1994.

Gardens and Chinese Culture, Wang Yi, Shanghai People's Publishing House, 1990.

The Spirit of Chinese Arts, Xu Fuguan, Chunfeng Literature and Art Publishing House, 1987.

Chan Buddhism and Taoism, Nan Huaijin, Fudan University Press, 1991.

Ancient Chinese Architecture, New World Press, 2004.

Wood Carvings of the Ming and Qing Dynasties, and the Republic of China, Dong Hongquan, Wanjuan Publishing Company, 2005.

The Art of Chaozhou Wood Carving, Zeng Qingzhao, Lingnan Fine Art Publishing House, 2004.

China's Dongyang Wood Carving, Hua Dehan, photos by Ren Jing, China Photography Publishing House, 2001.

The Art of Furniture Decoration in the Ming and Qing Dynasties, Pu Anguo, Zhejiang Photography Publishing House, 2001.

Chinese Decorations, Liu Senlin, Shanghai People's Publishing House, 2004.

Illustrations of Chinese Redwood Furniture of the Ming and Qing Dynasties, Yu Jiming, Zhejiang University Press, 2001.

Furniture of the Ming and Qing Dynasties, Cao Qianli, Zhejiang University Press, 2004.

Furniture of the Ming and Qing Dynasties, Zhu Jia, Shanghai Science and Technology Publishing House and Commercial Press (Hong Kong), 2002.

The Chinese Art of Root Carving, Xu Huadang, China Forestry Publishing House, 2005.

Rockeries in the Gardens South of the Yangtze River, Shao Zhong, China Forestry Publishing House, 2002.

Records of Construction of the Classical Gardens of Suzhou, China Building Industry Publishing House, 2003.

The Myth of Zheng He's Treasure Ships, Shi Hequn, Harbin Engineering University Press, 2005.

A History of Chinese Shipbuilding, Xi Longfei, Hubei Education Publishing House, 2000.

Five Thousand Years of China Illustrated, Xu Huping, Jiangsu Children's Publishing House, 2002.

Wood Carvings of the Han Dynasty, Zhang Pengchuan, Liaoning Fine Art Publishing House, 2002.

Furniture and Paintings, Hu Wenyan, Hebei Fine Art Publishing House, 2003.

Ancient Chinese Civilization Illustrated, People's Daily Publishing House, 1994.

Nomadic China, Xing Li, New World Press, 2005.

图书在版编目（CIP）数据

木头里的东方 / 石映照著；章挺权译. −北京：外文出版社，2006
（东西文丛）
ISBN 7-119-04458-3
I.木... II.①石... ②章... III.木材−文化−中国−英文
IV.S781
中国版本图书馆 CIP 数据核字（2006）第 049146 号

作　　者：石映照
责任编辑：崔黎丽
助理编辑：薛　芊
英文翻译：章挺权
英文审定：邵海明
封面及内文设计：天下智慧文化传播公司
制　　作：天下智慧文化传播公司
印刷监制：张国祥

木头里的东方

*

© 外文出版社
外文出版社出版
（中国北京百万庄大街 24 号）
邮政编码　100037
北京外文印刷厂印刷
中国国际图书贸易总公司发行
（中国北京车公庄西路 35 号）
北京邮政信箱第 399 号　邮政编码　100044
2006 年(小 16 开)第 1 版
2006 年 12 月第 1 版　第 1 次印刷
（英）
ISBN 7-119-04458-3
7-E-3716P